What people are saying about

FIELDS OF THE FATHERLESS

"*Fields of the Fatherless* was a moving and inspirational experience for me. Tom expresses many of the thoughts and beliefs that I share, and I pray that this little book finds its way into the hands of millions of Christians."

—Kay Warren, president of Acts of Mercy
and author of *Dangerous Surrender*

"In his life-changing book *Fields of the Fatherless*, Tom Davis shines a bright light on the true meaning of living out the gospel. His much-needed message reminds us of the urgency and frequency with which God commands His people to care for those who desperately need provision and protection. Based on a wealth of vital but often over-looked scriptural truth, this book is sure to surprise, challenge, empower, and ultimately bless you!"

—Heather Kopp, editor and best-selling author, and David Kopp,
cowriter of the New York Times best-selling *The Prayer of Jabez* and
Secrets of the Vine

"Tom has produced an interesting and compelling work that I hope finds its way into the hands of every Christian who is asking, 'How can I make a difference for God in the world?' Through *Fields of the Fatherless* you will look into the eyes of some beautiful but desperately needy children. Their stories will win your heart, and through Tom's wise direction, you will discover how to rescue theirs. This book is on my 'highly recommended' list."

—Chuck Smith Jr., founding pastor of Capo Beach Calvary and author
of *Frequently Avoided Questions: An Uncensored Dialogue on Faith*

"Tom Davis has written a heart-stirring book that is sure to be a wake-up call to all who desire to please God."

—Lisa Bevere, speaker and best-selling author of *Kissed the Girls and
Made Them Cry*

"As taught in the book of James, religion that pleases God is caring for orphans and widows. Christ said, '… whoever … gives to one of these little ones even a cup of cold water to drink, truly I say to you, he shall not lose his reward.' In this book, Tom Davis explains the why and the how to, and he and the Lord give us great encouragement to do it. Enough said!"

—Norm Miller, chairman of Interstate Batteries

"Tom Davis makes his case: We all can make a difference in the lives of the fatherless. What seems so daunting becomes so doable as Tom gently but insistently urges us to reach out to the lonely and the hurting—down the street and across an ocean. When we do just that, when we do reach out, our fear of getting involved with the fatherless quickly fades as we come to relish the privilege of reassuring young lives of our Father's unfailing love. Surely one reason Jesus taught us that it is better to give than receive is because, it turns out, giving is receiving."

—Dr. Mark Elliott, professor of history at
Southern Wesleyan University

"The story of the fatherless causes such a kaleidoscope of deep emotions because it is our own story. Our home is Eden, conversing with our Father, yet we all live far apart from the place and the parents we were designed for. Tom Davis provides us a mirror to our deepest pains and most powerful joys through the stories of amazing children and adults cared for by an even more amazing God. *Fields of the Fatherless* will move you to a life of deeper love and more urgent action."

—Brad Smith, president of Bakke Graduate School of Ministry

FIELDS

of the

FATHERLESS

FIELDS
of the
FATHERLESS

Discover the Joy of Compassionate Living

Tom Davis

x

David C Cook
transforming lives together

FIELDS OF THE FATHERLESS
Published by David C. Cook
4050 Lee Vance View
Colorado Springs, CO 80918 U.S.A.

David C. Cook Distribution Canada
55 Woodslee Avenue, Paris, Ontario, Canada N3L 3E5

David C. Cook U.K., Kingsway Communications
Eastbourne, East Sussex BN23 6NT, England

David C. Cook and the graphic circle C logo
are registered trademarks of Cook Communications Ministries.

LCCN 2008922801
ISBN 978-0-7814-4847-5

© 2008 Tom Davis
Published in association with the literary agency of Alive Communications, Inc,
7680 Goddard St., Suite 200, Colorado Springs, CO 80920

First edition published by Global Publishing Services in 2002 © Tom Davis,
ISBNs 978-0-9714100-1-5, 0-9714100-1-1

The Team: Andrea Christian, Steve Parolini, Amy Kiechlin, and Jack Campbell
Cover Design: The DesignWorks Group, Jason Gabbert
Cover Photos: Steve Gardner, PixelWorks Studios, Inc.; JupiterImages; Shutterstock

Printed in the United States of America
Second Edition 2008

1 2 3 4 5 6 7 8 9 10

022808

*To those God calls
"the fatherless," whose cries
are echoing across time. May
their lives be radically changed
because those calling upon the
name of Christ as Savior hear
their cries and are moved with
compassion to act.*

and

In Loving Memory of
GERALDINE ALICE BRANHAM

ACKNOWLEDGMENTS

There are some significant people whose kindness and graciousness have greatly contributed to the birthing of this book. My heart is overflowing with thankfulness for their effort and encouragement.

Don Pape—you have been more than a publisher and agent to me. It was your vision for this book and belief in its message that has brought it to this point. From the depths of my soul, thank you for being a good friend.

Andrea Christian—you have become such a good friend. I love your heart for the poor and oppressed. How many countries do you think we can travel to in the years to come?

Alive Communications—thanks to Rick Christian and Beth Jusino for believing in the message God has placed in my heart and for continuing to refine it!

I would like to especially thank my project manager of the first printing, Katherine Lloyd, who is a wonderful lady and a gift sent from above.

Eternal gratitude goes to my unsung hero, Heather Harpham Kopp, who personally sacrificed time and effort simply because she loved this project and has a huge heart.

Thanks to Holly Halverson for the hours of editing and reading that helped make this book a reality.

Without the inspiration of my good friend, Chuck Smith Jr., I'm not sure I'd have had the stamina to endure this undertaking. Thanks for your friendship and wisdom. You will always be special to me.

To George Steiner, Matthew Monberg, Samantha Kerr, and all of my colleagues at Children's HopeChest who continually labor beside me in the fields of the fatherless: Thank you. Visions aren't worth having if you see them alone. George, thank you for believing in me as you continue to see things in me that are hidden to the rest of the world. You are a true man of God who is Christlike in his every breath.

To Moira & Steve Allaby for sharing your adoption story through this book and for the many hours of help you so graciously provided to me.

To Garrett Chynoweth for sharing this passion with me and helping bear the burden of what it means to enter the heart of God and live what He lives. You are truly a man who has lived this principle and made a difference in many fatherless lives.

Brandon Chynoweth, thanks for the initial inspiration and ideas you've shared. You're a true brother.

To the rest of my close family, Lisa, Calvin, Uncle Paul, and Tyler—

you are all dear to my heart and examples of God's overwhelming love to the fatherless.

Thanks to Kevin and Jennifer Harrison who have a deep passion to make a significant difference in this world. They also reveal the true nature of Christ's character in their actions. Thanks for believing enough to sacrifice.

To my grandfather, Herb Branham. Had you not taken in a little boy who desperately needed a father I would not be where I am today. Thanks for being my dad and for surrendering your retirement years to raise me. Your legacy will live on through my life and the lives of my children.

My life and this book would not have been complete without the loving support of my wife, Emily. Sweetheart, you have truly been my source of inspiration and support. Thank you for giving me the confidence to be who God has called me to be. Thanks to the joys of my life, my sister-in-law, Hannah, my Russian "daughter" Lena, and my wonderful children, Anya, Hayden, Gideon, Scotlyn Grace, Lilly Joy, and Hudson for being patient with your daddy while he was writing and you wanted to play!

CONTENTS

FOREWORD

In the year 2000, my family's lives were changed forever through the miracle of adoption. Although we had fears and doubts, we stepped in faith, and adopted our daughter Shaohannah Hope from China. And so, our journey into the "fields of the fatherless" began. Since that time, we have adopted two more precious daughters from China, Stevey Joy and Maria Sue.

This little book, *Fields of the Fatherless*, is packed with biblical truth about God's heart for orphans. The Lord has told us that He is the Father of the Fatherless; so, if we truly want to experience God, we must go where He is—in the fields of the fatherless. It is in this place where God reveals Himself. In one of my recent visits to an orphanage in China, God showed Himself to me in another little orphan girl who lived without the love and hope of a forever family. When I looked at her, it was as if I saw the face of Jesus Himself.

As an adoptive father and one who has visited many orphans around the world, Tom Davis is a living epistle, showing to us God's call to the church to care for orphans in their distress. Tom shares with us testimonies of the fatherless and reveals the heart God has for them. It is my prayer that God will reveal Himself to you in the pages of this book and that you, too, will see the face of Jesus as you step in faith by answering God's invitation. I have more profoundly experienced my Savior through the miracle of adoption than in anything else.

As my wife, Mary Beth, so clearly put it, "When they handed me Shaohannah, God was more real to me in that moment than He had ever been. It about knocked me down!"

Whether this book is the first step of your journey into the fields of the fatherless or a stepping-stone along the way, I hope that as you read it, God's love and grace will become so real to you that you, too, would be "knocked down."

It's scary for me to think we might have missed all of this. In the next few pages, you'll hear about how true joy often hides in dark little corners, waiting for discovery. Mary Beth and I could have missed the joy of adoption by not seeking it out. Now, we look at our family, and we can't imagine missing something so key in what it means to walk close with God.

I want to invite you to experience the miracle! God has called us—your family and mine—to work together in bringing His love into this world. Right now there are millions of children around the world in need of a loving home. How are we—the church—going to respond to the heart of God to care for orphans? Search your heart, study the

Scriptures, and read this book. When you're done, I promise your life will never be the same. You'll step into the joy of God's miracle.

We are the hands and feet of our Savior. Will you join me? There are millions of orphans, single moms, widows, and strangers waiting to see that someone cares.

Fighting for the fatherless,
Steven Curtis Chapman,
recording artist

In this world you are an orphan—

  eagerly anticipating your adoption as God's child.

In this world you are a widow—

  longing for reunion with your Bridegroom.

In this world you are a stranger—

  a pilgrim waiting to become a citizen of heaven.

And in this world, God has called you to care for the orphan, the stranger, and the widow.

Fields of the Fatherless is a journey that brings you back to what Christianity is really about:

  Giving yourself to others

    Being Christ to a hurting world

      And living for the one that comes next.

INTRODUCTION

Holding Tight to Hope

My wife and I were flat broke. But we didn't care. If it truly was God's voice speaking to our hearts, if it truly was God telling us to adopt, we knew He would make a way, even if all the roads appeared unpassable.

The seed of our decision had been planted a few years earlier—the summer we led a youth-group mission trip to Vladimir, Russia, to minister to 150 orphans. For two weeks that summer, our lives were challenged in ways we never dreamed possible. Scripture came alive in ways it hadn't ever before. God spoke in tangible, palpable ways. The experience transformed the lives of every team member.

Especially ours.

And so there we were, broke and trusting God. That's the wonderful thing about finding yourself in a position where only God can provide—you have no option but to trust. He would have to provide the resources for us to bring this new little addition into our home; we couldn't.

I have a feeling you won't be surprised by what I'm going to say next ...

God *did* provide.

(Well, it was His idea in the first place, after all.)

We did our part too. This consisted primarily of sorting through mountains of paperwork and certified documents, making dozens of phone calls, and talking endlessly with INS (Immigration and Naturalization Service) officers. Eventually, we were ready to finalize the adoption of our little girl. Our adoption of Anya.

I flew to Russia in March to let her know the good news—we would bring her home in June.

I was tremendously excited, I felt like I was living in a dream. I couldn't wait to see this little fatherless girl and tell her she would have a family for the rest of her life.

Snow was falling in sheets, turning the dirty brown landscape into a cotton white winter wonderland. When our emerald green van pulled up to Yuriev Polsky on that cold spring day, I was bursting with anticipation to see my new daughter.

The orphanage was a dark, depressing place. Mortar spilled between the graying bricks of the exterior as evidence of careless construction or too many vodka breaks. The dimmest of lights peeked through windows, but there was no other sign of life. No one stood outside. No one greeted.

The building looked deserted.

I opened the creaky, oversized wooden door and stepped into a small foyer where I wiped my feet. Another door stared at me from the foyer.

One step through that threshold and I would see her—I would see Anya, the girl who would be our daughter. My heart was racing. What would I find inside? Would Anya say yes? Would she want to come home with us?

The staircase and hallway were lined with children. They stood against the walls, leaned on the railing, and crowded around the back of the room. Someone had alerted them about our visit. Hundreds of tiny eyes watched our every move.

A single lightbulb dangled high above our heads, bouncing odd shadows ungracefully round the room.

I looked at the children, they looked at me, none of us sure what to do. Like bullets, two little girls shot toward me at a hundred miles an hour. It happened so quickly, I didn't have time to react. One grabbed my right leg, the other, my left. They wrapped their arms around me and squeezed tight. I remember thinking how nice this was, these little girls showing me so much affection. I vaguely remembered seeing them at camp the previous summer but couldn't place their names. But my goodness, what sweet little girls!

Then one of them started rubbing my leg as if I were a favorite stuffed animal. Her big brown beautiful eyes looked up at me, and she started speaking. It was just one word, but she said it over and over and with every repetition, knives punctured my heart.

"Papa," she said. "Papa, Papa, Papa …"

I gasped. I wanted to say something, anything that would let her know she was special, that she *did* have significance, that she didn't deserve to be rejected.

But … she was not Anya. She was not the girl I would be soon calling my daughter.

All she and the other little girl wanted was the chance to have a family.

I can only imagine what went through their sweet little minds. The desperation, the hope, and the love they desired and deserved to have were all too much for me to process. I decided right then, in that orphanage, that I would do whatever I could to help orphaned boys and girls around the world who were hoping against hope that someone would love them. I knew I couldn't adopt seventy children (although it did cross my mind), so what could I do?

I made a commitment to help the organization that exposed me to the needs of Russia. I called my friends, raised money, and took countless trips, all in an attempt to do whatever I could to help orphans like the two little girls who wouldn't let go. That very year, my church sponsored an entire orphanage of kids. The programs we helped establish gave them a hope and a future.

Today, I travel the United States, Canada, Europe, all over the world doing whatever it takes to bring awareness of the orphan's plight to the body of Christ, the secular world, to whoever will listen and has a heart to help the least of these. Why? Because they're worth it. Every little boy or girl who sits alone, feeling rejected and abandoned by the world, deserves to know they have a Father in heaven who loves them ... and that there are other people with skin on who love them too.

God has a passionate love

> *God has a passionate love for the fatherless of our world—the people He calls widows, strangers, and orphans.*

for the fatherless of our world—the people He calls widows, strangers, and orphans. Our involvement, our engagement in the lives of the fatherless can reap huge benefits in their lives. We are Jesus' hands and feet, and the world is waiting to see us in action.

Perhaps your path will be through adoption, but there are many other ways to respond—through advocacy, sponsorship, letter writing, taking a trip to visit orphans, or starting a group that's committed to making a difference in your community.

But whatever you do, do it now because those two precious girls weren't just holding onto my legs—they were holding tight to hope.

You can give it to them.

CHAPTER ONE

The Fields

What am I missing?

Some years ago, I found myself asking this question almost daily. As a pastor, I thought I knew what mattered to God. I read my Bible almost every day. I tithed, I watched the "right" movies, I prayed as often as I could. I kept my devotions on track and I even journaled in an attempt to reflect on what was happening in my life!

But none of this could shake my conviction that I was still missing something.

Something important.

That question eventually led me on the mission trip to the Russian orphanage, where the two little girls who desperately clung to my legs brought me the answer.

God showed me two life-changing truths during this time. It is these truths that began to answer my question, "What am I missing?"

> I sensed God loving these kids directly through me.

The first truth was how deeply in love God is with the poor and the outcast. I didn't just learn this truth intellectually, I *felt* it. Throughout my stay, I sensed God loving these kids *directly through me.*

The second truth was how much God blessed me—how much joy He desired to give me—when I participated with Him in doing something that mattered so much! I had never before experienced God's pleasure and approval as strongly as I did in Russia.

That experience started me on a path of discovery in God's Word. It was a search that yielded surprising truths about the life God promises to bless—and about a special group of people.

The People on God's Heart

If you searched the Bible from front to back, you'd find many issues close to God's heart. But you'd also notice three groups of people that seem to come up again and again.

Allow me to introduce you to those people God wants us to put at the top of our priority list: the orphans, widows, and aliens (strangers). These are the weak, the underprivileged, and the needy among us, and they all have a desperate need of provision and protection.

Scripture mentions the importance of caring for these individuals more than sixty times! Clearly, the protection and well-being of these people is one of God's great and constant concerns. He actually defines who He is by His promises to them.

Consider His promise to provide:

> *A father of the fatherless, a defender of widows,*
> *Is God in His holy habitation.*
> *God sets the solitary in families;*
> *He brings out those who are bound into prosperity.*
>
> (Ps. 68:5–6)

His promise to ensure justice:

> *He administers justice for the fatherless and the widow,*
> *and loves the stranger, giving him food and clothing.*
>
> (DEUT. 10:18)

His promise to bless those who bless them:

> *At the end of every third year you shall bring out the tithe of your produce of that year and store it up within your gates. And the Levite, because he has no portion nor inheritance with you, and the stranger and the fatherless and the widow who are within your gates, may come and eat and be satisfied, that the LORD your God may bless you in all the work of your hand which you do.*
>
> (DEUT. 14:28–29)

Many other passages, including Isaiah 1:17, Psalm 82:3–4, and Zechariah 7:10, confirm God's commitment to this special group.

The Ancient Boundary

It shouldn't surprise us that God would take direct action to ensure His intentions for the fatherless were carried out. God commanded His people to set aside a portion of their fields for the sole purpose of providing for this group. The line that designated this special area was called the ancient boundary. It created a field, figuratively and literally, in which the alien, orphan, or widow could find the provision necessary to survive.

> *You shall not pervert the justice due an alien or an orphan, nor take a widow's garment in pledge. But you shall remember that you were a slave in Egypt, and that the LORD your God redeemed you from there; therefore I am commanding you to do this thing. When you reap your harvest in your field and have forgotten a sheaf in the field, you shall not go back to get it; it shall be for the alien, for the orphan, and for the widow, in order that the LORD your God may bless you in all the work of your hands. When you beat your olive tree, you shall not go over the boughs again; it shall be for the alien, for the orphan, and for the widow. When you gather the grapes of your vineyard, you shall not go over it*

again; it shall be for the alien, for the orphan, and for the widow. You shall remember that you were a slave in the land of Egypt; therefore I am commanding you to do this thing.

(DEUT. 24:17–22 NASB)

This passage opens with a call to biblical justice. While that may not be a particularly popular topic for a Sunday sermon, God is very concerned with justice, specifically when it involves the lives of people who suffer. Here, justice means taking care of the physical needs of aliens, orphans, and widows. It means taking passages to heart that talk about what justice looks like, like this one:

We know love by this, that He laid down His life for us; and we ought to lay down our lives for the brethren. But whoever has the world's goods, and sees his brother in need and closes his heart against him, how does the love of God abide in him? Little children, let us not love with word or with tongue, but in deed and truth.

(1 JOHN 3:16–18 NASB)

Oh, we've done it so many times haven't we? Though we have the means necessary to help someone in need, instead we shut down our hearts and let stinginess get the best of us. Here's my confession: "I'm

> *When it comes to caring for the people on God's heart, indifference is a sin.*

guilty of this!" We all are. But we can't let ourselves repeat these patterns. We need to hear God's truth in a fresh way, and in a way that trickles through our lives and into our actions.

We are also all guilty (by association) of living in a fallen world. It's a world that tries to press all of us good Christian folk into a mold shaped by self-concern, routine, conformity, and hypocrisy. However, living Jesus' way demands that we turn our back on our natural inclinations. Instead of self-concern, we need to be more concerned with loving our neighbors as ourselves and taking care of their needs. Instead of conforming to what every other Christian does and what society wants us to do, we must lay down our lives and allow our actions to speak louder than our words. The primary place this happens is in our love for other people. That's the life Jesus calls us to live more than any other.

One of the best definitions of *justice* I've heard is implied by the definition of its opposite: *evil.* Edmund Burke, an eighteenth-century British philosopher, said this: "The definition of evil in the world is when good men and women see injustice and do nothing." Here's another way to look at it: When it comes to caring for the people on God's heart, indifference is a sin.

The Deuteronomy 24 passage goes on to remind the Israelites that they were once slaves. We, too, were once slaves: slaves to sin ("dead in [our] trespasses and sins" is how Ephesians 2:1 [NASB] phrases it). We had no hope; we were slaves with no way out. In the same way God delivered the Israelites out of their bondage, he also delivered us. Romans 8:2 goes on to say that "the law of the Spirit of life in Christ Jesus has made me free from the law of sin and of death."

Thank God we were set free and that we're no longer slaves! What an incredible picture of the love and goodness of Jesus. What greater gift could there be? God wants us to remember our bondage, remember how He has saved us, and in that remembrance, He wants us reach out in love to the fatherless. That's what it means to be grateful.

The rest of the Deuteronomy passage would have spoken powerfully to the Israelites. While we may take food for granted today (it's only a short drive to the grocery store), everything the Israelites did revolved around seedtime and harvest.

What God was saying to the Israelites was simple: Harvest your fields without delay and enjoy the goodness you've worked hard for. But don't think only of yourselves. You know all that excess you have lying around? The extra sheaves, the olives that remain on the trees, the grapes still on the vine? Leave that for the widow and orphan, and you'll be blessed. This wasn't just a passing thought, it was how God's people were supposed to live their lives.

And it's also how He wants us to live ours.

Do you have lots of material goods? Share them with those who have little. It's really that simple.

Pure Religion

Some might be tempted to presume that God's principle about a special field for the poor was just a quaint, ancient tradition—that it's irrelevant today. Yet we clearly see in the New Testament that God's passion for the poor, parentless, and alienated transcends time. His words concerning those in need are every bit as urgent in the New Testament as in the Old.

The apostle James wrote that caring for orphans and widows is the very essence of religion:

> *Pure and faultless [religion] is this: to look after orphans and widows in their distress.*
>
> (JAMES 1:27 NIV)

Acts 6 records an incident that exemplifies how the early church lived out God's command to take care of the poor. When the number of disciples was increasing, the Grecian Jews among them complained about the Hebraic Jews because their widows were being overlooked in the daily distribution of food. So the Twelve gathered all the disciples together and said, "It would not be right for us to neglect the ministry of the word of God in order to wait on tables. Brothers, choose seven men from among you who are known to be full of the Spirit and wisdom. We will turn this responsibility over to them and will give our attention to prayer and the ministry of the word" (vv. 3–4 NIV).

This proposal pleased the whole group. They chose Stephen, a man full of faith and of the Holy Spirit, and six other men. They presented these men to the apostles, who prayed and laid their hands on them (see Acts 6:1–6).

What's important to note about this passage is that the apostles were the ones who were handing out the food! This was not a task to be swept under the table (no pun intended). Why? Because the apostles knew "pure religion" meant ministering to those widows. They understood that such service was God's heart! At the point it became too overwhelming because of the numbers, they found men "full of faith and the Holy Spirit" (v. 5), laid hands on them, and appointed them to the task.

If the early church spent so much of its time focusing on the fatherless in this respect, shouldn't we make them a priority as well?

God gave us the responsibility to care for the defenseless. It's through our hands the Father's love touches, it is through our voices His voice is heard, it is through our efforts and those of the church that His care is revealed to the ones the rest of the world has forgotten.

> *Pure and faultless religion is this: to look after orphans and widows in their distress.*

The Church in Action?

The church is not an institution consisting of walls and stained glass. The church is people; people who represent the physical body of Christ on earth. We as the church are called to put flesh to His words and make Him alive to those who are desperate to know He is real.

In recent years, ministering in the fields of the fatherless hasn't been as much of a priority to the church as it has been throughout history. Many well-intentioned believers have lost sight of what God cares about most. The fact is, we put most of our energy into improving what is inside the four walls of our churches rather than bringing in the harvest that is outside.

A good friend once asked me, "If the fields are white for harvest, why do we spend all of our money on painting the barn?"

Ministry to Christ's body is important, but when we don't balance it with a legitimate attempt to care for the fatherless in our communities and around our world, something is terribly wrong.

The statistics reveal our neglect. When I originally wrote *Fields of the Fatherless* in 2002, reports indicated that there were over 70 million orphans in the world. Today, there are over 143 million according to the UN Statistics Division. *That's one child in every thirteen.* More than 13 million orphans were added to that total in 2006 alone, many of these due to the ravages of the HIV/AIDS pandemic. Every 5 seconds a child dies because he or she is hungry; 10.9 million children under the age of 5 die in developing countries every year—malnutrition and hunger-related accounting for 60 percent of these deaths. More than 1 million children are trafficked every year as sex slaves and another 8.4 million children work under horrific circumstances—forced into debt bondage or other forms of slavery, prostitution, pornography, armed conflict, or other illicit activities. By the end of 2006, there were 2.3 million children living with HIV around the world, and over half a million children became newly infected with HIV in 2006.[1]

Yet a 2001 Barna Research Group poll revealed a telling statistic: Evangelical Christians are less likely than are non-Christians to give money and assistance to AIDS-related causes. Only 3 percent of evangelicals say they plan to help with AIDS internationally as opposed to 8 percent of non-Christians.[2] This is only one example of how Christians have let down in their love for the unlovely.

This is not God's way. If we are to please Him, we must recover what has become a lost cause—the fatherless.

The encouraging news is that loving a person in need is much easier to do than you might think. You don't have to become a mission-

> *"If the fields are white for harvest, why do we spend all of our money on painting the barn?"*

ary or take a vow of poverty to reach out to the people on God's heart. You can participate in some very practical ways and make differences that will last an eternity.

As you meet the fatherless in these pages, you will be surprised how simple it is to make a dramatic change in a human life. You will learn how you can give just a little bit of God's love to someone else and watch him or her transform. You will discover abundant joy for your efforts, as well as something you might not have anticipated.…

The Promise of a Blessing

Of course we should not care for the fatherless because of what we might get in return. Loving others isn't a 401K or an investment program! Yet don't miss this: There is a valuable blessing in store for those of us who actively care for the fatherless.

Remember the passage in Deuteronomy 24? God blesses those who leave the food for the widows and orphans.

God's blessing was not something the Jewish people took lightly. God's blessing enabled them to defeat their enemies. God's blessing prospered them and formed them into a great and mighty nation. The blessing of the Father meant the difference between success and failure, prosperity and poverty, abundance and want.

What about the church today? The blessing of the Lord is our inheritance:

> *Finally, all of you be of one mind, having compassion for one another; love as brothers, be tenderhearted, be courteous; not returning evil for evil or reviling for reviling, but on the contrary blessing, knowing that you were called to this, that you may inherit a blessing.*
>
> (1 PETER 3:8–9)

In both the Old and New Testaments, this word *blessing* connotes an infinitely lovelier circumstance than our word *happiness*. Happiness is temporal. It's a thing of chance and luck, a gambler's paradise. But the biblical word for *blessing* has to do with significantly satisfying fruitfulness. Blessing is the

When we pay attention to the treasures of God's heart, we put ourselves in a position of blessing.

roses around your lawn, the beauty of fresh-fallen snow on the mountainside, and spontaneous blasts of joy. God's blessing is not just a
nice thing to have; it's a necessity for those who desire to walk in genuine satisfaction.[3]

The Hebrew word for *blessing* is *baruch*. It implies being hunted
down and pursued by the favor of the Lord.

That is how much God desires for His people to be blessed!

The blessing God poured upon His people was one that affected
"all the work of [their] hands."

It meant not only favor for the nation, but also favor for the indi-
vidual. The same is true today. God promises that if we take care of the
needs of the fatherless, whatever we put our hand to will be blessed:
our work, the home we build, and the relationships we hold—even the
families we lead. When we pay attention to the treasures of God's heart,
we put ourselves in a position of blessing.

I have seen this in action. From the moment we understood God's
passion for the fatherless, my wife and I made it a priority to care for
them. It never ceases to amaze me how God blesses our lives when we're
ministering in these fields.

Let me give you an example. After doing what we could to help the
fatherless by building relationships with kids from broken homes at
our church and giving financially to some orphanages overseas, we
decided to take our care one step further. Remember Anya? This little girl in a foreign country
genuinely moved our hearts,
and we decided to adopt her.
I've already mentioned our
financial obstacle: We didn't

> *God always provides when*
> *we desire to help!*

have enough money to complete the adoption. We felt we had a promise from God—we trusted that He would provide. We knew His blessing rested on those who cared for the fatherless.

Two weeks before the adoption was final, we still didn't have the funds. Some days we were tempted to panic because time was short, but by the time we boarded the airplane to go pick up our new daughter, we had received more than ten thousand dollars from friends and others we didn't even know.

That's the provision of God in action. And it's part of the benefit that comes with ministry to the fatherless. God always provides when we desire to help! Proverbs promises that "he who has pity on the poor lends to the LORD, and He will pay back what he has given" (19:17).

You will receive a lifelong blessing when you follow the instructions of the Lord and join Him at work in His favorite fields.

NOTES FROM THE FIELD

I hated my life since the third grade when I was unmercifully beaten. I felt then that life is lost and death is looking for me. And my tears were telling me that life was nothing in comparison with death. I felt like a little cockroach, which [responds in] fear when seen.

A bunch of American people came to our school. I thought these people wanted to laugh at us. But I mistaken. They are people willing to give up the most precious gift a person can possess, love. [Their] intentions to share seemed strange as they had their own kids. But these people have such big hearts to give that there is still enough room even for us little cockroaches.

Then I began to feel myself not a cockroach anymore that deserved to be killed, but a little human being. It is a wonderful feeling. Believe me.

—FROM A RUSSIAN ORPHAN

CHAPTER TWO

The Fatherless

One of the things I often hear when I travel and speak at different churches and conferences is, "Jesus said we'll always have the poor. So, no matter what we do, there will always be poor people." Hmm ... is that supposed to be some kind of acceptable excuse to go about our lives in comparative luxury while the rest of the world starves on less than a dollar a day?

Why do so many of us look for the easy way out, for a way to be let off the hook rather than living out of our compassion? Listen, I'm guilty of this too. I like my life just like it is. I don't like it when the status quo is interrupted in any shape, form, or fashion. "If you would just leave me alone I'd be fine." But I don't stay long in this place. Once the words of Scripture are illuminated, the truth of what they say doesn't allow me to make excuses. This issue of how to treat the poor is something we *have* to pay attention to.

Take a look at Deuteronomy 15. This is where you'll find the origin of the "we'll always have the poor" statement Jesus references in his teaching.

> *If there is a poor man among your brothers in any of the towns of the land that the LORD your God is giving you, do not be hardhearted or tightfisted toward your poor brother. Rather be openhanded and freely lend him whatever he needs. Be careful not to harbor this wicked thought: "The seventh year, the year for canceling debts, is near," so that you do not show ill will toward your needy brother and give him nothing. He may then appeal to the LORD against you, and you will be found guilty of sin. Give generously to him and do so without a grudging heart; then because of this the LORD your God will bless you in all your work and in everything you put your hand to. There will always be poor people in the land. Therefore I command you to be openhanded toward your brothers and toward the poor and needy in your land.*
>
> (DEUT. 15:7–11 NIV)

"If there's a poor man among you …"? Goodness, we don't have to look for the poor. In our great big shrinking world, they're everywhere: when you cross the street, when you turn on the TV, when you go downtown, when you read a book (like this one, for example), so what are we supposed to do with them?

That's the big question. Do we have permission to blow them off? Are there any reasonable excuses why we *shouldn't* help them? Verse 8 says we are to be openhanded and freely give whatever that fellow needs. That's not the easiest thing in the world to hear. Like many of you, when I hear that I'm also looking for a back door to sneak out of this responsibility. God won't let me. I *have* to freely give. Reminds me of another verse I don't like to remember:

> *Freely you have received, freely give.*
>
> (MATT. 10:8)

That's a difficult Scripture to read. And even more difficult to live out. It is a reminder of what I'm truly supposed to be doing while visiting this planet. We could continue to dance all around this issue, but let's not. Let's just get right to the heart. It's helpful to remember that God is always about blessing people who bless the poor. "That's how He rolls," as my kids would say. But the bottom line of this principle is found in verse 11. Yes, we will always have the poor with us, so then what? Are we supposed to ignore them, hope for the best, walk on the other side of the road? No. We're supposed to open our hands to them. God puts the poor in our lives so we will reveal compassion. It's a test for us and a promise to them. Are we passing or failing?

> God puts the poor in our lives so we will reveal compassion.

Jesus said we would always have the poor among us, so the question we need to answer is, who are the needy today? And how do we apply the ancient commands to twenty-first-century living?

I don't know about you, but I don't have a few hundred acres of farmland out back to share with the fatherless! What I do have is what those fields represent.

In a biblical culture, people lived by the sweat of their brow. As we saw in the last chapter, they made their living by growing grains, fruits, and vegetables, as well as tending livestock. Today our jobs and businesses are our livelihoods. They give us the harvest we have to share with the fatherless.

What do the fatherless look like today? We can all picture the unforgettable sad-eyed orphans and the poverty-stricken Haitian kids with their distended stomachs, but what about those in our daily world?

Perhaps they look like ...

- The widower at church who always shares candy with the squirrelly kids
- The girl who babysits your children and has no father at home
- The single mom next door who always seems to be harried—in and out of her car with kids, groceries, and work-related paraphernalia
- The unruly little boy in your child's class who keep getting moved from foster home to foster home
- The lonely college student waiting for the bus every day as you pass by
- The grandma who lost her husband ten years ago and spends her days watching soap operas
- The little girl who in Africa who has to sell her

body for a loaf of bread because she's starving to
death

- The prostitute in Russia who knows no other way
to live because both of her parents died and nobody
would take her in

It's More Than Money

Right about now you might be
thinking, "This book isn't for
me! I don't have any money to
give. I barely make ends meet as
it is!"

Let me assure you that lack of
funds doesn't disqualify you for
service in God's fields. As you'll

> *The needs of the
> fatherless aren't only
> financial.*

read in a moment, the care we're talking about goes way beyond money.
Yet too often I've noticed people using their own limited means as an
excuse for doing nothing.

Another objection I often hear is this: "Wasn't welfare created to
help the poor?"

Well, setting aside the larger issue of global poverty for a moment,
it's a fair question. But welfare is something that man's wisdom designed
to provide for those in poverty. Without getting into the problems the
welfare system has generated, I think it's important to note that it is
not a biblical idea.

According to the Bible, the needs of the poor are to be absorbed into society. The needs of the fatherless aren't only financial, so throwing a check at the problem once a month is *not* the answer. The fatherless have social, emotional, and spiritual needs money alone can't solve.

This is where you and I come in. This is where we live out the command of Matthew 10:8. Not only by providing a portion of our "fields" financially, but also by giving of our time and our talents to enter into the lives of the suffering—to walk among them and give them hope and a future.

Ruth and Boaz

The Bible records a beautiful picture of redemptive caring that's as powerful as any contemporary example I could find. It's found in the book of Ruth, chapter 2.

Ruth and her mother-in-law, Naomi, are in a state of despair. Both are poverty-stricken and hungry widows. They decide to travel to the land of Naomi's ancestors, the Israelites. The problem here is that Ruth, a Moabitess, is considered an enemy of the Jewish people.

When they arrive, Ruth realizes their hope lies in a field of the fatherless.

> *"Let me go to the fields and pick up the leftover grain behind anyone in whose eyes I find favor." ... So she went out and began to glean in the fields behind the har-*

vesters. As it turned out, she found herself working in a
field belonging to Boaz.

(RUTH 2:2–4 NIV)

How Boaz treats Ruth is a perfect picture of how God's people are
to respond to the fatherless. Take a look at how the story unfolds. Boaz
takes special notice of Ruth working in his fields. He welcomes, affirms,
and blesses her.

The LORD repay your work, and a full reward be given
you by the LORD God of Israel, under whose wings you
have come for refuge.

(RUTH 2:12)

Boaz takes further steps to protect her. He tells her,

Do not go to glean in another field, nor go from here,
but stay close by my young women. Let your eyes be
on the field in which they reap, and go after them.
Have I not commanded the young men not to touch
you?

(RUTH 2:8–9A)

Boaz provides for Ruth.

When you are thirsty, go to the vessels and drink from
what the young men have drawn.

(RUTH 2:9B)

Then Boaz honors her by inviting her to his table.

> *Now Boaz said to her at mealtime, "Come here, and*
> *eat of the bread, and dip your piece of bread in the vine-*
> *gar." So she sat beside the reapers, and he passed parched*
> *grain to her; and she ate and was satisfied, and kept*
> *some back.*
>
> (RUTH 2:14)

Boaz is sensitive to the position she is in and respects her. He tells his men,

> *Even if she gathers among the sheaves, don't embarrass*
> *her. Rather, pull out some stalks for her from the bundles*
> *and leave them for her to pick up, and don't rebuke her.*
> (RUTH 2:15 NIV)

And finally, the ultimate honor, Boaz makes Ruth part of his family.

> *So Boaz took Ruth and she became his wife.*
> (RUTH 4:13)

Each step Boaz makes toward Ruth is the epitome of how Christ wants to appear to the world! Let's see how God manifested his unconditional love through Boaz:

- *He treated her with respect even as He acknowl-*
  edged her need—Today's poor feel embarrassed,

down-trodden, maybe even bitter. They need to be
treated as equals.

- *He provided for her*—No one should be without
  adequate food, shelter, and clothing. These basic
  necessities give a person worth so they can be open
  to receiving the love God has for them. As God
  directs, we make our "fields" available as resources
  we can provide from.

- *He affirmed her*—The fatherless have been lanced
  with the pain of rejection and the anxiety of loss. A
  kind, affirming word will remind them of their
  value and has the same result as pouring water on
  dry, thirsty land.

- *He protected her*—Protecting people in need means
  being their advocate. Stepping in to meet a need is
  a form of protection, but just being a friend can give
  the assurance of protection from loneliness, hunger,
  fear.

- *He honored her*—What a statement it makes to
  invite a person in need to sit at your table and treat
  him or her as family.

- *And finally, the ultimate redemption: God, through
  Boaz, made her family*—Redemption means salvation, deliverance, and rescue. When we become
  redeemers like Boaz, we can even play a role in helping those in need see Jesus, perhaps even to discover
  their own relationship with God. What greater gift
  can we offer than Jesus Himself?

The Justice Due Them

Job, one of the most righteous men who ever lived, committed his life
to share what he had with the fatherless. When he asserted his integrity
before God, he described the big picture of what we should all hope to
achieve for those in need:

If I have denied the desires of the poor
or let the eyes of the widow grow weary,
if I have kept bread to myself,
not sharing it with the fatherless—
but from my youth I reared him as would a father,
and from my birth I guided the widow—
if I have seen anyone perishing for lack of clothing,
or a needy man without a garment,
and his heart did not bless me
for warming him with the fleece from my sheep,
if I have raised my hand against the fatherless,
knowing that I had influence in court,
then let my arm fall from the shoulder,
let it be broken off at the joint.
For I dreaded destruction for God,
and for fear of his splendor I could not do such things.

(JOB 31:16–23 NIV)

Job's everyday life illustrated how to make sure the fatherless received
what they needed—from fair treatment in court to clothing to fatherly
guidance.

And isn't it interesting that when God talks about this group, He repeatedly uses the term *justice*?

In the last chapter, we read that God commands us not to "[distort] the justice due an alien, orphan, and widow" (Deut. 27:19 NASB). But what is the justice due to them? What rights do they have, and what provision can they expect from those who claim to be God's followers?

The truth might surprise you. God doesn't consider our caring response to the plight of the needy as "optional" or merely a nice gesture. He sees a loving response to this group as a complete and preordained human right—a legal right backed not by an earthly court but by the very halls of heaven!

> *The sure way to deprive the poor of justice is to do nothing.*

To deprive the fatherless of justice doesn't simply mean denying them a proper hearing in court. It means *not* welcoming them into your home, *not* helping them when they are cold and hungry, *not* listening when they cry out. In other words, the sure way to deprive the poor of justice is to do nothing.

The apostle John suggests "doing nothing" is proof that God's love doesn't abide in us:

> *But whoever has this world's goods, and sees his brother in need, and shuts up his heart from him, how does the love of God abide in him?*
>
> (1 JOHN 3:16–17)

James says if we see someone in need and give only lip service to caring for him or her, our faith is worthless.

> *What does it profit, my brethren, if someone says he has faith but does not have works? Can faith save him? If a brother or sister is naked and destitute of daily food, and one of you says to them, "Depart in peace, be warmed and filled," but you do not give them the things which are needed for the body, what does it profit? Thus also faith by itself, if it does not have works, is dead.*
>
> (JAMES 2:14–17)

I believe when you strip Christianity down to its basics, this is what it means: to feed, clothe, and treat the fatherless as members of one's own family.

How do we do this? In chapter 5, I'll share practical ways to make a difference in the lives of the needy. But for now, meet a few of the fatherless who found God's love through His followers.

The Fatherless Among Us

Emily

In her early childhood, Emily had everything most of us could ever want: a loving mother, a picture-perfect father, a beautiful home in an upper-middle-class neighborhood, and five brothers and sisters to love and to fight with and make lasting memories. Emily had no warning life was about to deal her a devastating blow.

June 27, 1988, began like any other morning. Emily was just a month away from becoming a teenager. School was out for summer, and it was a perfect day for hanging out with friends and running through the water sprinklers to get some relief from the humid south Texas heat. Dad was off to work, and Mom was running

> *She desires to help others realize their tremendous value to their true Father.*

errands with the younger ones, while the older kids tackled a different adventure.

Later that morning, a man walked into the family-owned appliance shop where Emily's father worked. He shot Emily's father multiple times. It was a hate crime committed by a member of the extended family that took away the life of a loving father long before his time.

Sadly, this was just the beginning of a tumultuous time for Emily. The nature of the crime and the murderer behind it meant the family had to enter the Witness Protection Program. They took assumed names and moved to California, away from friends, family, and everything they knew as home.

After this series of traumatic events, Emily's mother, Lillian, became distraught and spiraled into a deep depression. She was admitted to a psychiatric hospital while a friend tended the children.

After undergoing intense counseling and treatment, this young mother of six was released from the hospital.

The hospital staff failed to tell anyone in the family that Lillian was on heavy doses of medication that could result in severe mood swings. Early the morning after Lillian came home, Emily woke to the sound of a gunshot. She ran into the living room with one of her brothers and discovered their mother's lifeless body lying on the living-room floor.

Tragically, all six children were now orphans, left alone in the world to fend for themselves. Emily, Brandon, Lisa, Garrett, Hannah, and Calvin had become sojourners in the fields of the fatherless.

Fortunately, a couple named Bob and Phyllis adopted all six children and kept them together as a family. God's grace has been clearly revealed because a couple stepped out of their comfort zone and ministered the love of God to wounded children. They are all changed forever because people cared.

I know all this because Emily is my wife. Instead of being bitter about her past, Emily is one of the most loving people I know. She continually sacrifices her time and resources to support the fatherless. Do you want to know why? Because she has been fatherless. She knows the life change that occurs when love is given. Her own loss helps her be responsive to others in similar situations. She desires to help them realize their tremendous value to their true Father.

Tom

I, too, have been one of the fatherless. I met my real father only a few times during the first sixteen years of my life. My mother married the proverbial "wicked stepfather," a career military man with a strong love for the bottle and not much else.

When I was eleven, my mother decided to leave my stepfather for the fifth of seven times. I had been attending a little church in town and was involved in the junior high youth group. I went to church more to get away from the house once a week than I did to learn about God. I would have done just about anything to get out of the hellish home environment—it was a miserable place. But God pulled a fast one on me. He used a painful time in my life to reveal His love for me through someone's caring concern.

I had nobody else to talk to about the circumstances facing me, so I told the youth pastor, Kurt. I didn't know him very well, but to my surprise he responded with a huge amount of love and affection! He offered to

> *God used a painful time in my life to reveal His love for me through someone's caring concern.*

pick me up on the next Saturday to take me out to eat and to the park with his family. I became a member of his family for a day.

And what a day it was! I never felt so loved, so cared for, and like I actually mattered. I certainly didn't feel that way in the place I was forced to call home. Our "family times" were nothing at all like the time I spent with Kurt's family. Our "family times" were defined by drinking, cussing, yelling, and various forms of physical and verbal abuse. I could count on that menu for breakfast, lunch, and dinner.

But on that special Saturday, Kurt treated me like his own child. He took me on a picnic, bought me ice cream, and played soccer with me.

They were simple acts of kindness, but they made a profound impact on me. Kurt had absolutely nothing to gain personally. He just poured out biblical, selfless love to a little boy who desperately needed it. I had never felt such genuine love from anyone in my entire life. That experience changed me!

My mother and I packed everything we could into a motor home and left early that following Monday morning. I wound up in Midland, Texas, living with my grandparents.

A few short weeks later I found myself in another church, but this time I wasn't there merely to escape a difficult home life. This time, I heard the message of Christ's love and I gave my life to Him. I surmised that if the love Christ had for me felt anything like the kind of love Kurt and his family gave me, I certainly wanted more of it—every day for the rest of my life.

> *It was the kind of love that changes a life.*

Though I never was truly an orphan by the technical definition of the word, I surely had felt like one. I had been desperately lonely and believed nobody loved me. But on one Saturday in June, a kindhearted man and his family showed me the simple beauty and immense power of true, unconditional love. I will never forget that day.

Angie

Angie is a single mother of three. Like thousands of other women across the country, she was abandoned by men who told her they loved her, then left after the birth of their child.

The needs Angie has are practically overwhelming. She has medical bills, a need for child care while she works, then there's rent, food, clothing, a car payment, gas—anyone would agree this is an enormous burden for one person to bear.

Angie's life changed dramatically when a few people made the decision to respect her and love her unconditionally. Hers is a beautiful story of the church being Jesus: People gave money to help furnish her apartment, provided bags and bags of groceries, stepped in to watch the kids so she could go to work or just take a break. They showed the kind of love that changes a life.

Because of their help, Angie was able to go to Bible school. Because of their help, she got a job teaching kids how to be gymnasts. And now she is also leading a ministry to help others in the neighborhood the way she was helped! Because a few people stepped boldly and generously into the fields of the fatherless, Angie has come to know Jesus and to share His love with others. Just as Ruth was redeemed from her past, Angie has exchanged her burdens for freedom.

Are you beginning to see the life-changing impact you can have when you reach out with God's love to someone who otherwise feels unloved or abandoned? Think about the boy or girl in your neighborhood who is a member of a single-parent home who may need the love you have to give. Think about the widow at church who may need your financial aid or the warmth of a family.

Your love in a fatherless person's life can transform that person's current reality and eternity. It did for me. That's why treating the fatherless like members of your own family is so important to God. It's the only way they'll ever know His love for them—through you.

The Inspiration: Gratitude

The issue of thankfulness is yet another principle revealed in Deuteronomy 24. This isn't just another principle; it's why we do what we do.

> *Remember that you were slaves in Egypt, and the LORD*
> *your God redeemed you from there. That is why I com-*
> *mand you to do this.*
>
> (DEUT. 24:18 NIV)

In other words: *Remember where you came from.*

The idea of remembrance was deeply embedded in the Jewish culture. One example of this is Passover, which is an event celebrating Israel's redemption from slavery in Egypt. Every time a Jewish family sits down for Passover, they remember where they came from and how God delivered them.

> *Freely you have*
> *received, freely give.*

Can you remember what it was like to not know the peace of God— to face your days alone? Remember when you didn't have that reassurance of salvation—when there was no hope for eternity? Remember how the Lord found you, had mercy on you, and saved you?

Peter reminds us of a time when you and I were not the people of God, a time before we found His love. Our gratefulness ought to be a wellspring that pours out the same kind of freedom and joy to others.

> *But you are a chosen generation, a royal priesthood, a holy nation, His own special people, that you may proclaim the praises of Him who called you out of darkness into His marvelous light; who once were not a people but are now the people of God, who had not obtained mercy but now have obtained mercy.*
>
> (1 PETER 2:9–10)

It is essential for us to feel the gravity of this kind of love and forgiveness, because it is out of this understanding that we learn to be merciful toward others. Remember that verse in Matthew: "Freely you have received, freely give" (10:8)? Because of Christ's love for us, because He forgave us such an enormous debt we could never repay, we can show others the forgiveness and love of Christ.

Genuine, believing faith manifests itself in tangible ways when we care for those who are poor, suffering, and fatherless or motherless. Your gratitude will make you sensitive to the needs of others—you can't help but feel compassion and act on it.

> *The man with two tunics should share with him who has none, and the one who has food should do the same.*
>
> (LUKE 3:11 NIV)

What Jesus is saying in this verse is that we should all give out of our abundance. Listen, if you don't have two coats, don't worry about giving one away. Enjoy the one coat you do have. But if you're like many Americans, your problem isn't that you don't have two coats, it's that you have five. Or ten. That puts a greater sense of responsibility on us.

> *From everyone who has been given much, much will be demanded; and from the one who has been entrusted with much, much more will be asked.*
>
> (LUKE 12:48 NIV)

This is another one of those verses that chafes a bit. Of course it does so in a good way, challenging our modus operandi. How I do life may not always be the way I'm *supposed* to be doing life. If I'm living in comfort and blessing, more is required of me as a follower of Christ. Ouch. Here's the bottom line of this truth: My "blessings" are opportunities for me to reveal the reality of the faith I proclaim to possess. It's the proof in the pudding of my beliefs.

I know that we all have a tough time with these kinds of things. They're not easy, especially when contemporary Christianity leads us to believe the lie that our faith was all about *our* comfort. That's not how life worked out for Jesus, the apostles, or any of the heroes and heroines of the faith.

The great news is that a sacrificial life is the freest way to live. A sacrificial, giving life is a life filled with the most meaning and significance. And it's the life Jesus blesses. There's no guessing or hoping for blessing; it simply comes because He's true to His word.

And so here's the question we must wrestle with: Will we dive into the deep waters of God's presence, or will we be content to swim in the shallows where all the flotsam and jetsam live? The choice is ours....

NOTES FROM THE FIELD

I was a single mom needing to move to another town for job reasons, but I couldn't afford to hire movers. I knew I couldn't possibly load and unload a U-Haul by myself.

Yet I couldn't bring myself to ask friends for help. After all, everyone knows what kind of hard work and hassles moving involves.

A couple weeks before the move, I bumped into a friend who knew of my plans. When she offered to help, I assumed she was just being polite. "Well, maybe. I'll let you know …"

But she insisted. "My boyfriend and I are going to help you move next Saturday."

"Really?" I asked.

She said, "Yes, we are." Just like that. Later that week she called to ask what time they should come over on the day of the move.

My friend's decisiveness was just what I needed. People may not realize how hard it is for single moms to ask for help—or even to receive it when it's offered! Thank you, dear friends, for insisting and for taking the time out of your own busy Saturday. I'm learning that there are people who truly want to help, and I'm discovering I can let them.

—FROM A SINGLE MOM IN OREGON

CHAPTER THREE

What Does God Look Like?

Is it possible for a man or woman to look into the face of God and live? Historical accounts in the Bible tell us that only one man was privileged to actually see God. In Exodus we find out God spoke with this man "face to face, as a man speaks to his friend" (33:11). The inevitable result: He was distinctly marked forever. His name was Moses.

Being in God's presence had a powerful impact—it literally changed Moses' physical appearance. His face was shining so brightly, he had to put a veil over it. The glory of God was so strong, the people couldn't bear to see it.

But then, as written in the New Testament, God became man. He took up His residence in human flesh as Jesus, and came to live among us. The mystery of all mysteries! As fully human and fully

God, Jesus Christ walked on this earth. Mankind was finally able to see God *face-to-face*, and those who saw Him were, like Moses, marked forever. Jesus said, "He who has seen Me has seen the Father" (John 14:9 NASB). Seeing God by being with Jesus—what an incredible gift!

Have you ever experienced a spiritual event that was so real, so dramatic, it changed who you are and how you live? One of those defining moments when you knew you touched the eternal?

I remember such an event when I was in high school. It wasn't even the happening that was so profound; it was the message it brought me.

I finally had what every sixteen-year-old dreams of: the coveted driver's license. Although the car my grandfather bought wasn't exactly the car of my dreams—a fifteen-year-old Buick Regal with a second-rate paint job—at least it was drivable. But most important, I was the driver.

One horribly humid Texas summer day, I was on my way to golf practice. I lived with my grandparents in a fairly affluent community where neighbors were usually helpful to one another. But on this day, everyone's Southern hospitality must have been played out.

As I turned a corner, I saw some commotion about a half-mile ahead of me on the side of the road. An older woman was standing by her car, trying to flag someone down. The two cars in front of me drove right past as if they saw nothing. But I pulled over.

After I climbed out of my

> *God became man, took up His residence in human flesh as Jesus, and came to live among us.*

car, I realized what this woman was so frantic about. She had been trying to get her elderly mother into her wheelchair, when the attempt
went haywire and her mother fell over. The poor woman was lying
along the side of the road, and the wheelchair had fallen on top of her.
Several attempts by her daughter to get her back into her chair had
failed miserably.

The helpless woman was nearly hyperventilating because she was so
upset. I lifted her off the ground, settled her comfortably into the chair,
and wheeled her safely into the
house.

Those two women were so
thankful! They thought I was
the most darling young man in
the world and were ready to
nominate me for Citizen of the
Year. The daughter said they'd
been there for more than thirty

> *I left there feeling on top of
> the world! I had done
> something to help someone
> who was in need.*

minutes, trying to get someone to pull over and help them. Everyone
was just too busy.

I left there feeling on top of the world! I had done something to
help someone who was in need—someone who was entirely helpless
without my assistance. But I also felt something else: I felt like I had
done something special to please the heart of God—that He was smiling at me and enjoying my meager efforts.

I think for the first time in my life I saw the face of God—I saw it
in that elderly woman who was lying on the ground in need of someone who would show her compassion.

My actions that day thrust me into the realm of the eternal.

Jesus Is Very Near

You may be wondering, *How could you possibly see the face of God in an elderly woman on the side of the road?* Allow me to explain. Or better yet, let Jesus explain.

In Matthew 25, Jesus paints a remarkable picture of what the end of the world will be like, and what will happen at judgment. In doing so, He reveals the importance of our actions on this earth and how they will affect our eternity. Beginning in verse 31, Jesus returns in all of His glory to separate the sheep from the goats—the true believers from the false believers. After the division, He tells the sheep—the true believers—to enter the kingdom of God He has prepared for them since the beginning of the world. And then He tells them why they are able to enter:

> *For I was hungry, and you gave Me something to eat; I was thirsty, and you gave Me something to drink; I was a stranger, and you invited Me in; naked, and you clothed Me; I was sick, and you visited Me; I was in prison, and you came to Me.*
>
> (MATT. 25:35–36 NASB)

> *Whatever you did for one of the least of these brothers of mine, you did for me.*

The righteous who are listening to Jesus are confused. They can't think of a time when they did any of this directly to Jesus. How can you minister to Jesus and miss it? His answer is found in verse 40. "I tell you the truth, whatever you did for one of the least of these brothers of mine, you did for me" (NIV).

Suddenly their eyes are opened. When the righteous gave to others, they were giving to Jesus. *Wow! If that's the reason Jesus gives for ushering us into His kingdom, it is surely a powerful statement as to what He's looking for from us.*

What Jesus didn't say is almost as important as what He did say. He didn't say, "Whenever you help the successful people or the truly religious people, you're helping me." No, the people Jesus was referring to were down-and-out, people who couldn't care for themselves, the helpless, the needy. Ministering to these people, Jesus said, is equal to ministering to Him.

This passage of Scripture reveals the heart of our Lord. He aches for those in pain, He sees the needs of the hungry and hungers with them, He hears the cry of the orphans, identifies Himself with their misery, and lowers Himself to their level.

In his book *Something Beautiful for God*, Malcolm Muggeridge gives a meaningful picture of what this service looks like in one of us. His example was the late Mother Teresa, who unarguably gave her life to loving the people Jesus loved most. He described her as a woman

> with this Christian love shining about her; in her heart
> and on her lips. Just prepared to follow her Lord, and
> in accordance with His instructions, regard every
> derelict left to die in the streets as Him; to hear in the
> cry of every abandoned child, even in the tiny squeak
> of the discarded fetus, the cry of the Bethlehem child;

to recognize in every leper's stumps the hands which once touched sightless eyes and made them see, rested on distracted heads and made them calm, brought health to sick flesh and twisted limbs.[1]

This is a key to understanding the passage in Philippians that describes Jesus as suffering servant:

> *[Jesus,] who, being in the nature God, did not consider equality with God something to be grasped, but made himself nothing, taking the very nature of a servant.... He humbled himself, and became obedient to death— even death on a cross!*
>
> (2:6–8 NIV)

> *He left the beauty and perfection of heaven to be identified with all people.*

Jesus, in order to reveal His love to creation, left the beauty and perfection of heaven to be identified with all people. In other words, He emptied Himself of all that He was, in order to be one of us. He became part of humanity—became our brother. You see, we *all* are the least of these!

We have a tendency to look at passages like this in the Bible and say, "Oh, those poor dears: hungry, thirsty, sick, and needy." But that's the great paradox! That's exactly who we were before Jesus found us! We are all the same at the core.

And because He has poured out such love and care for us, we are to go find "the least of these," and do the same. The truth is, we see Jesus in the eyes of the poor *because we see in them who we really are*. We are able to have genuine compassion as Christ has compassion on us— because we see ourselves.

Remember how in the beginning we spoke of the joy that occurs when we participate in helping those whom God cares about most? I'd like to think about that again for a minute.

You may be saying, "I would love to help the fatherless, but it is so heartbreaking!" Well, guess what ... true joy doesn't always come through the things that give us warm fuzzies.

Despite what Jesus knew He would have to go through with dying on the cross, He trusted in what God wanted Him to do. He saw the bigger picture. It's difficult to grasp, but the reward that will come far outweighs any of the uncomfortable feelings we may have. So we

> *fix our eyes on Jesus, the author and perfecter of faith, who for the joy set before Him endured the cross, despising the shame, and has sat down at the right hand of the throne of God.*
>
> (HEB. 12:2 NASB)

Did you see that? For *the joy* He knew was coming, He gave Himself. We, too, can look forward to the joy God promises as we help others find God's love through the giving of ourselves.

God's Face Today

So what does God look like?

He looks like the Romanian orphan who doesn't have a hope in the world unless someone enters his life and reveals to him the love of the Father.

Oh, look! Another glimpse of God.

He looks like the little girl in Africa who has no father, who has watched her mother's body being ravaged by AIDS for the last five years, and has been crying over and kissing her since she took her last breath about ten minutes ago. Now she has nobody, she's only seven, and she's standing all alone on a dirt road as they carry her mother away.

He looks like the struggling single mother who is hanging on by an emotional thread. She is mother, father, protector, and provider, and to top it all off, she has to leave the child she loves so much in the hands of a stranger all day, just so she can work and put food on the table.

Oh, look! Another glimpse of God. Do you see Him in the eyes of that young Palestinian student who just left his family to study in America? He's isolated, a stranger, and in need of someone to show him what the real love of God feels like.

Yes, Jesus looks a lot like these people. Will you look for His face in all the people you see today?

Jesus is hungry. Jesus is thirsty. Jesus is naked. Jesus is in prison. Jesus is sick. Will you do what it takes to minister to Him? For the joy set before you ... search for the treasure in earthen vessels. When you do, you'll find Christ Himself.

NOTES FROM THE FIELD

It always puts a smile on my face to think of the days when I met you. Most of all I remember the moment when you told us about the Lord. I know if He helped you, He will help me, too.

I was put in the foster-care system when I was three. Everyone loved me when I was small. I took joy in life. Then the years started going faster and faster. I was a big girl already. Good days are always over at some point. Everyone left me, my brothers, my sisters. I was left alone.

Then my life stopped. I kept seeing my relatives in my dreams. I quit sensing, playing the guitar, everything. But then you came into my life. When you told me about Jesus, I came back to life ... I think God will help me to find my sister. I pray He'll help me to get to know Him better....

Love, Katie

—FROM A YOUNG GIRL IN FOSTER CARE

CHAPTER FOUR

The Blessing of Adoption

I do a lot of public speaking, and whenever I mention the word *adoption*, I get two very different responses. The response from the adoption crowd—people who have already adopted or hope to adopt someday—is one of joy, wonder, excitement, and thankfulness, while the nonadoption group act puzzled, uncertain, nonchalant, or disdained. Amazingly, I see this second response even from pastors when I tell them I'll be talking about adoption to their congregation. I think they're afraid I will alienate most of their parishioners. And perhaps I *would* alienate them if I spoke about only the world's definition of *adoption*.

But I don't. I talk about the biblical definition of *adoption*.

Adoption Is God's Idea

Adoption was not something man created to solve the problem of orphans in a fallen world. Before time as we know it began, God had the idea of adoption in His heart.

> *He predestined us to adoption as sons through Jesus Christ to Himself, according to the kind intention of His will, to the praise of the glory of His grace, which He freely bestowed on us in the Beloved.*
>
> (EPH. 1:5–6 NASB)

I love this verse because it tells us quite clearly that adoption was part of God's original design. God saw our need to be part of a family, an eternal family, and He responded. Our adoption into God's family is the greatest thing that could happen to a human being. It offers answers to the greatest questions man has asked: "Am I alone in the universe?" "Am I abandoned?" "Is there life after death?"

> *When we are adopted into God's family through faith, we know that we will never be alone.*

When we are adopted into God's family through faith, we know that we will never be alone, that we have a Father in heaven who loves us, and that eternity is only the beginning of our lives.

I'm reminded of the last words of Dietrich Bonhoeffer, a martyr for the Christian faith during the time of World War II. As he was being taken from the prison in Flossenburg to be hanged on the gallows, these were his last words: "This is the end. But for me, it is the beginning of life."

Bonhoeffer knew that leaving this life was just the start of an amazing eternal future. And he understood that what made this possible was his adoption by God into the kingdom. What a wonderful gift.

Adoption and the Holy Spirit

When we receive Jesus as our Savior, one of the gifts we receive is the gift of the Holy Spirit as Peter communicated in the Acts 2:38 (NIV):

> Peter replied, "Repent and be baptized, every one of you, in the name of Jesus Christ for the forgiveness of your sins. And you will receive the gift of the Holy Spirit."

One of my favorite things to study in Bible school was the Holy Spirit. Not just because He's powerful and mysterious, but also because of what the word really means. In the Greek, the word for the *Holy Spirit* is

> *The fact that the Holy Spirit is in our lives confirms that we are sons and daughters of God.*

parakletos, which means "helper, advocate, or the one who comes alongside of another."

The "orphan spirit" inside each of us that tells us we're alone, unworthy, or unloved is healed by the presence of the Holy Spirit. He leads us, guides us, and protects us just as a physical mother and father would do with a child. Can you see the correlation here? The fact that the Holy Spirit is in our lives confirms that we are sons and daughters of God and gives us the right to call God our Father.

> *For all who are being led by the Spirit of God, these are sons of God. For you have not received a spirit of slavery leading to fear again, but you have received a spirit of adoption as sons by which we cry out, "Abba! Father!" The Spirit Himself testifies with our spirit that we are children of God.*
>
> (ROM. 8:14–16 NASB)

Adopting a Child

If we truly believe that human beings are created in the image of God, this forces us to place a high value on human life. Every child deserves to be raised in a loving family environment with a mother and father. It was never God's original intention for millions of orphans to be sharing beds in crowded institutions or sleeping alone somewhere on the African prairie. No. This is a result of man's fallen nature and evil manifesting itself on the earth and destroying the very fabric of the family.

I've already mentioned how many orphans there are in the world as of this writing. Here's that number again: 143 million. I know that seems like a lot, but not compared to the number of professed Christians living on the earth. That number is 2.1 billion. There are 159 million people who claim to be Christians in the United States alone. I know you see where I'm heading, but is it so far-fetched? With so many Christians in the world, is it so far out of the realm of possibility to imagine every one of those orphans being adopted into a family just as God has adopted us? If only 7 percent of professing Christians around the world responded, every single orphan in the world would have a home.

I love what John Piper says about adoption. He believes adoption is the "visible gospel." In other words, the adoption of an orphan into a family perfectly illustrates what God did for us in sending His Son, Jesus. As the Talmud says,

> *A mother is likened unto a mountain spring that nour-*
> *ishes the tree at its root, but one who mothers another's*
> *child is likened unto a water that rises into a cloud and*
> *goes a long distance to nourish a lone tree in the desert.*

People seek to adopt children for many different reasons. To some, the idea of adoption comes as naturally as breathing. To others, it comes over time or through an experience: a mission trip overseas or walking with friends or family through the adoption process.

While every adoption experience is unique, one word seems to speak to the ways in which children and families are brought together: *convergence*. I believe once people open or lend themselves to the idea of adoption, God works in miraculous ways to bring about the desire of His heart: the grand orchestration of setting the loneliest of His children in a loving, caring family.

> *Stepping into the fields of the fatherless opens a new way of thinking about what it means to accept, to love, and to parent.*

All orphans, all children, deserve to have loving families. Unfortunately, many cannot be adopted. In some countries, no infrastructure exists for such a process. In other cases, it is simply more feasible to support orphans through programs in their countries, such as sponsorship. This is not a bad thing—I have seen God's powerful hand touch the lives of orphans through people who give and pray and correspond with them consistently. Though this may not be the ideal, it is sometimes the best possible option in our broken world.

I can tell you firsthand, and from talking to hundreds of people who have adopted children, stepping into the fields of the fatherless opens a new way of thinking about what it means to accept, to love, and to parent.

I've included two adoption stories here because they convey what so many tell me about adopting: God makes special provision for orphans. Blessing comes with them and follows them, because they are close to God's heart. When you extend your heart to the fatherless, you give blessings, and you are blessed. This does not always mean this is an easy or straightforward process, or that the parenting comes easy—it's often just the opposite.

Coming to Adoption

Moira and Steve's Story

Moira: I had always thought I would like to adopt a child. I was adopted by my father when I was eighteen months old, and I don't believe a better man walks the planet. But when I got the urge to become pregnant, the Jaws of Life could not pry this thought from my mind. For seven years, I asked God why He, who created the universe and breathed the breath of life into the first human being, couldn't do this one very small thing for me. As far as I could tell, He wasn't answering.

[My husband,] Steve, was open to the idea of building our family through adoption sooner than I was. He waited for me to come along.

> Then I prayed the scariest prayer of my life: "God, I'm giving you my desire to have a child."

In spring 2001, I was driving home down the familiar road that led to our street, and I could sense God, or some polite and persistent messenger from that realm, breathing over my shoulder. I had sensed this before, and I knew this presence wasn't leaving anytime soon.

I said out loud: "Okay! I'm finished with it." Then I prayed the scariest prayer of my life: "God, I'm giving you my desire to have a child. Let your will be done in my life."

I opened the door to adoption, and Steve was ready, so we talked, researched, and prayed for direction. Domestic adoption? Less expensive than most foreign adoptions, but risky, especially for people who had just spent seven years in a cycle of hope and disappointment. Foreign adoption was costly and had its own set of uncertainties.

Soon after, I talked with a woman who had adopted two daughters from China through a local agency. It was through talking with her that God gave us the marching order we were waiting for: "China." Steve and I attended the adoption orientation. The agency was started by two Chinese nationals, a brilliant husband and wife, who were living in the United States. The husband led that night's presentation. He spoke about the one-child policy in China, a "don't ask, don't tell" policy of abandonment, and tens of thousands of babies, mostly girls, in need of loving parents. That night, the thought of our daughter began to take root in our hearts. We were overcome with emotion. We never could have anticipated the events that would unfold, bringing us not one child, but two.

Melody and Matt's Story

Matt: In August 2007, Melody and I left church, and she said to me, "Matt, during the service God showed me a picture of a child from Ethiopia and impressed upon my heart that we are supposed to adopt a daughter from Ethiopia." Like a key turning a lock, my spirit was in total agreement. I didn't doubt or flinch. I knew that the time had come. The green light was here.

Africa was not a surprise to us. Thirty years ago, Melody was born in Jos, Nigeria. Her parents were missionaries with SIM [Serving In Mission, out of Charlotte, North Carolina] and were actually married in the field in Nigeria. Melody spent most of her growing-up years in Liberia before moving to Kenya for high school. We met at Wheaton College, and in 1997 we visited her family in Addis Ababa, Ethiopia. That was my first trip to Ethiopia.

Once we got married, we immediately started discussing adoption. It was always something we both wanted to do, and felt called to. However, the timing was never quite right. We did not see that "green light" from the Lord. In the meantime, we became surrounded by adoptive families. Our church home group alone had four adopted children in it! (Our two kids were the only biological children.) There are at least a dozen

> We prayed that God would provide comfort and a sense of security to our daughter until we could take her in our arms.

families—close friends, work colleagues, friends from church—who have adopted and have been part of our journey toward adoption. We had gotten close in the past, but it never quite came together. We knew the time had come.

Practical Considerations

Moira and Steve's Story

Moira: At the time we considered adoption, we lived in a 630-square-foot house on two acres of land. We were both self-employed. This was not the glowing picture of prosperity we knew we needed to impress the Chinese Center of Adoption Affairs. We leveraged, had some money set aside, and prayed for God's provision. What we didn't expect was that we would face two adoptions in the span of a year. Yet we moved forward, and God provided—even to the tune of a $10,000 check. We have talked to many other families who experienced the same type of miracle in the midst of their adoption process.

As we prayed and waited, we wondered if our child had been born yet. Did she feel wanted? Was she still with her birth family or at an orphanage? People who adopt from China talk about the red thread that connects adoptive families to their children before they have the opportunity to meet. We prayed that God would provide comfort and a sense of security to our daughter until we could take her in our arms.

Melody and Matt's Story

Melody: Since Matt and I have officially begun this adoption process, I have been processing the impact a third child will have on our family. I carried my children, Caroline and Tobin, in my body. I was their protector, their provider, and their comfort for those nine (make it ten!)

months. I was the first person to see them come take their first breath (well, me, a nurse, a doctor, and Matthew). I was there those first days of their lives and beyond. In my limited experience, all that I mentioned above is what I defined as motherhood.

With our third child, our daughter from Ethiopia, my definition of *motherhood* has to be different. I'm selfishly grieving that I won't be those things to her. Someone else will have the privilege of carrying her throughout her first months of life. Someone else will give birth to her. Someone else will care for her during those first few days. My journey of motherhood with our third child, our daughter, will begin when she is handed to me, when I take her in my arms.

There is a part of my heart that is empty right now. I know that I have another child, a daughter, who is waiting for me. Instead of caring for her by eating right, exercising, not gaining the usual fifty-plus pounds, I must instead pray, dream, and wait. So I'm trying to use this time to dream about what this new type of motherhood will be. Instead of newborn moments, I will have other times with her. I will laugh, love, and care for her as my daughter brought to me by God, not of my flesh but of my heart.

Convergence: The Hand of God

Moira and Steve's Story

Moira: Just after we sent our dossier to China, ready to wait and prepare to meet our daughter, we were approached about another adoption. A fifteen-year-old who was pregnant was looking for parents for her child. After prayer and with caution, we moved forward with her and her boyfriend. We went to doctors' appointments and talked about the open relationship that would ensue after the birth. Yet we had a sense all along that we were on a bit of a risky venture. We were not wrong.

I've never been one to see spiritual messages in the steam from the shower or hear the voice of God in my dreams. But one day in late November when I was reading my Bible, God spoke to me.

When Steve came home that evening, I told him, "I have a strong sense that this adoption is going to fall through, but we are supposed to move forward with it anyway." I said, "God has a baby for us, and it's a boy," and I shared this verse that God gave to us, Isaiah 42:16: "I will lead the blind by ways they have not known; along unfamiliar paths I will guide them; I will turn the darkness into light before them and make the rough places smooth. These are the things I will do; I will not forsake them" (NIV).

The day she called to say she was keeping the baby, God was with me. He helped me measure my voice as I said, "Yes. I'm not surprised. What's your plan? Do you have everything you need?"

Two days later, Steve and I drove down the mountain to return the baby items that this fifteen-year-old had given to us. She delivered that evening. It was a girl. I remember saying to Steve, "You see, a girl. That child was not for us." And though we had faith in God, still we were crushed.

One Sunday in late December, we were again approached, this time by a man and woman whose daughter, we learned, was twenty and pregnant. She lived in Kansas and was planning on giving her baby up through adoption. Did we think we'd be interested in writing her a letter, introducing ourselves as prospective parents?

My answer: "No, thank you." The baby was due in March. This young woman was already connected with a family in Kansas who wanted to adopt her child. Odds didn't seem in our favor.

Then the couple said, "We believe you are supposed to be the parents of our grandchild. Can we pray with you?"

So they prayed. My emotions were raw from our recent experience, and I wept uncontrollably. Steve and I left that day in a tailspin.

I told him in the car, "I'm not doing this again."

He said, "What harm can it do to write a letter and send a few pictures?"

So I picked up some of what we'd written for the past two adoption attempts, and I sent them to the birth mom in Kansas. This young woman called us to say that she had already chosen a family. I appreciated the call. Chapter closed.

On January 27, 2002, we got word that this young woman in Kansas had her baby. There were medical issues and the other couple backed out. Were we interested in adopting this child?

I sat down on the kitchen floor to process this information. The baby had been born prematurely. Medical issues. It was a boy. I remembered God's words: "I will lead the blind by ways they have not known, along unfamiliar paths I will guide them."

When Steve walked in the door, I said, "This is the one. This is our boy."

A series of miracles brought us to Kansas to meet a perfect-looking five-pound, seven-ounce blond-haired baby with double dimples and a cherubic mouth, our son Spencer.

On December 10, 2002, just before Spencer's first birthday, the phone call came. The voice said, "You're pregnant!" It was the referral person from our Chinese adoption agency telling us the code words we understood to mean we had received our match. This was earlier than expected. She gave us some information and our daughter's birth date: February 15, 2002. She and Spencer were just twenty days apart.

That afternoon, Spence, Steve, and I drove to the agency to see the picture of our baby girl. She had huge dark brown eyes that seemed to hold a world of sorrow. Then we saw another picture where she was tearing up the place, apparently flinging large toy letter blocks about. We've come to see that both aspects speak to our daughter's character.

Through God's gracious provision and direction, we prepared to travel in February with a group of eight other families, just after celebrating Spencer's first birthday, to pick up our daughter. Her Chinese name was Yao Yao, meaning distant. We gave her the name Olivia Bo Allaby. *Bo* means "precious treasure," and it is the name she goes by today.

I started to laugh at how God was so clearly orchestrating all of these moves at just the right time.

Melody and Matt's Story

Matt: We had made our decision, but we didn't know much about Ethiopian adoption agencies. So I Googled "Ethiopia Adoption." The first link that came up was for America World Adoption Association. AWAA is a partner of the organization I work for, and we know their leadership well. I was excited, and sent off an e-mail to a friend there. I said, "This is probably not your area, but can you tell me about your Ethiopian adoption program?" He wrote back and said, "Actually this is my area." I was stunned again and took it as another confirmation that we were walking in God's will.

The next "coincidence" was with our home study agency in Castle Rock[, Colorado]. I got an e-mail from a good friend—someone who the organization I work for had interviewed for a job—and she had just accepted a position with Hope's Promise: our home study agency! I started to laugh at how God was so clearly orchestrating all of these moves at just the right time.

Desire Fulfilled: Life on the Other Side

Moira and Steve's Story

Moira: We cherish the way our children came to us, but as miraculous as their arrival into our life as a family, that beginning is merely a shadow compared to the parenting. We found out after our daughter joined our family that she had severe-to-profound hearing loss in both ears. We were sad for her and disappointed, but we weren't distraught. Our adoption journey and time with Spence, through six surgeries, therapy, and countless doctors' appointments, gave us the fortitude we needed to say: "She's not hearing: What do we do?" Our children, their needs, and our adoption experience have opened up not only the typical world of parenting, but have introduced us to communities that have enriched our lives immeasurably. Adoption opens not *a* world, but *the* world. We had the privilege of being a part of something so incredible, we still cannot believe it happened to us. When we look into the faces of our children, now five, we cannot stop saying thank you.

> *I'm looking forward to being part of this club called "adoption."*

Melody and Matt's Story

Melody: It seems that for most of my adult life, I've tried to figure out what I say to people who are obviously a blended/adopted family. Do I ask them where their child is from? Would that be offensive? I know they know they look different, but I was never sure what to say, what to ask.

I'm looking forward to being part of this club called "adoption." Every time I see a family that has obviously adopted (and there are many families out there who don't "look" blended but are!) I try to figure out some way to tell them we're adopting right now. I felt the same when I was pregnant. I wanted to tell everyone that I was pregnant … and was thrilled when I began to show that pregnancy. That's how I feel now. We are having our third child. I no longer feel awkward asking questions. For me, I feel that I finally belong in a club that I have always wanted to be a part of.

And that club is exclusive … because I have already seen all the work it takes to be part of it. I never in my life imagined how *hard* it is to wait—for the government to process my paperwork, for the agency to come and make sure my home is fit for a child, for a referral that gives me a picture of my daughter. I am proud to be part of this club … and I cannot wait to be that blended family that stands out!

CHAPTER FIVE

Seeds of Hope

Take a moment to consider the lowly seed. One of the most amazing things about a seed is the mystery of how something so small and seemingly insignificant can turn into something so big, beautiful, and full of life.

My boys and I contemplated this a few days ago. We live in Colorado, and the growing season in this part of the country is very short. As we were enjoying a rare 72-degree day, my boys and I took on the tricky task of April seed planting.

They couldn't believe how tiny the seeds were! My oldest son said to me, "Dad, that seed is so small, nothing could grow from it. I can't even see it to plant it in the soil!" What a perfect time for a father to teach his son about how something inconspicuous can turn into something great; how just a little effort of planting in the spring can bring a wealth of flowers to enjoy all summer long, along with tomatoes, cantaloupe, and other yummy things to eat. My son is still having a hard time believing those seeds will actually turn into those things, but he says he'll take my word for it.

The Power of Planting Seeds

Many of the most significant outcomes in our lives are the result of someone having planted a seed. Think of the things that would never exist if someone hadn't started the process. Every beautiful piece of art, every major historical monument, the homes we live in, and everything humans have created started with the seed of a small thought and grew into reality.

> *One of the most significant seeds we can plant is the seed of hope.*

One of the most significant seeds we can plant—especially in the life of someone who is fatherless—is the seed of hope. A field will never produce a crop without the planting of seeds. And hope is *vital* to a person's survival, especially when the odds are stacked against him or her.

A true story about the power of planting seeds is told in Ken Gire's book, *The Weathering Grace of God*.[1] It comes from a man named Jean Giono, who tells of his encounter with a shepherd in the French Alps. At the time, deforestation had almost completely destroyed the land. The mountains and valleys were barren, the wildlife had deserted the area in search of greener pastures, and villagers had abandoned their homes because their springs and brooks had run completely dry.

While mountain climbing in this ravished area, Giono came to a shepherd's hut, where he was invited to spend the night. During their conversation, he learned that the fifty-five-year-old shepherd, Elzeard Bouffler, had been planting trees on the barren hillsides for more than three years. That evening Giono watched Bouffler meticulously sort through a large pile of acorns and pick out one hundred of the best seeds. It was a rather mundane task nobody would notice and even care about. Yet during those three years Bouffler planted 100,000 seeds, 20,000 of which had sprouted.

After World War I, Giono returned to the same mountainside where he had met the shepherd years earlier. The area looked entirely different. Where there was once a barren and deserted land were now the beginnings of a living, vibrant forest! A chain reaction in nature was occurring: Water flowed in the once-empty brooks. Meadows, gardens, and flowers were birthed where once complete desolation ruled.

Giono again returned to the French Alps after World War II. This time he found the shepherd continuing the thankless task twenty miles from the front lines. A vigorous forest, inhabited by farms and families, now

> *One person has the ability to completely revolutionize the life of an abandoned child, a foreigner, a single mom, or an elderly widow.*

covered the originally empty hillside. The beauty of the land had been restored for everyone to enjoy.

All of this took place because of the effort of one man planting seeds.

Where everyone else saw stripped hillsides devoid of any value, a shepherd saw the hope of seeds being planted that would one day bring back the beauty and glory the land once possessed.

One person has the ability to completely revolutionize the life of an abandoned child, a foreigner, a single mom, or an elderly widow. Your creative energy could be the very thing that helps him or her keep going and even experience God's love for the first time.

Will you just look at the devastation around you and find another place to make your home, or will you plant seeds of hope in lives that have been stripped bare by the misery of this world? The choice is yours.

When I'm Weak

Earlier I mentioned the staggering numbers of oppressed children in our world today. Here is another alarming statistic: The number of single-mother households with children under the age of 18 has remained at 9.8 million since 1995. Today there are 11.6 million single-mother households with children under 21. In 1998, 26 percent of all families with children were single-parent families.[2]

Now consider this: "Almost 70 percent of young men in prison grew up without fathers in the home."[3]

The need to reach out to the alien or stranger in our own country is also great: "A record total of 547,867 International Students [lived] on U.S. campuses for the year 2000–2001. [In addition] enrollment rose 6.4 percent—the largest increase since 1980."[4]

That's just the number on campuses! Just think of how many others are here from foreign countries, working or attending high schools in international exchange programs.

The fields of the fatherless are full to the brim with needy people. After reading these kinds of statistics, you may be asking, *What difference can I possibly make?* This was my question too.

A rather old, somewhat quirky story speaks to this issue.

A young man collecting seashells noticed an aged fellow walking along the beach. He saw this old man walk a few steps, bend over, pick something up, and fling it into the sea. He repeated this over and over.

Filled with curiosity, the young man moved closer until he realized what the old man was doing. He was picking up one of the many starfish that lay dying on the beach and throwing them far into the water.

> *Each of us can do something to alter the life of at least one person whom God loves and cherishes.*

The young man thought this task was an incredible waste of time. He asked, "Sir, why are you taking the time to try to save one starfish when there are thousands lying on the beach? You can't possibly make any difference!"

The older man smiled, bent over, picked up another starfish, and flung it into the ocean. Then he said, "It made a difference to that one!"

This simple illustration teaches us the importance of one action. We may not be able to do everything, to save all of the fatherless in the world—this I grant you. But each of us can do something to alter the life of at least one person whom God loves and cherishes.

Feeling too weak to make a difference, too empty of resources, or too fearful to try are normal human responses. I'm so glad for promises like the one offered in 2 Corinthians:

> "My grace is sufficient for you, for power is perfected in weakness." Most gladly, therefore, I will rather boast about my weaknesses, that the power of Christ may dwell in me. Therefore I am well content with weaknesses ... for Christ's sake; for when I am weak, then I am strong.
>
> (12:9–10 NASB)

We can step out, believing in God's strength to help us.

We *can* rely on Him to use impossible-looking situations to bring about the possible!

Personal weakness provides a great opportunity for God's strength to come through. He's just waiting for us to call upon Him in our weakness so He can show Himself strong on our behalf.

We need to change our minds about how we approach the things we fear (more on this in the next chapter) and the places in our lives where we feel weak. We can step out, believing in God's strength to help us, instead of letting our limitations defeat us. Then we can confidently join Paul and actually boast in our weaknesses because that is when God is about to show His power.

Every Seed Counts

A few years ago, I was visiting an orphanage and looking for a little friend I had made previously at summer camp. Having been in almost every nook and cranny of the orphanage trying to find Mark, I resigned myself to the fact that he must be somewhere in the city. But there, hunched down in the corner of the last room I entered, I found him.

When I said his name, he looked up, and I noticed two things. One, he had a nasty shiner on his left eye. Two, he was reading a Bible someone had given him at camp. We never did find out what happened to Mark's eye—he wouldn't say. But we did discover that, in spite of his current circumstances, Mark was finding comfort and solace in the Word of God.

> *Right there in the middle of the orphanage, a tree was sprouting and promising fruit that would last forever.*

Someone's little act of giving Mark a Bible—that seed—was a relatively easy and inexpensive thing to do. And yet do you see what was happening? Right there in the middle of the orphanage, a tree was sprouting and promising fruit that would last forever.

One day, there will be a forest in Mark's life, a forest that began with a single seed planted by someone who took the time to care. Someone like you or me.

Or George.

George's Story

I could tell you dozens of inspiring real-life stories of men and women who have followed God's call and affected thousands—not just heroes who come from our rich history of faith, but modern heroes too. One modern-day hero of mine is George Steiner.

After the fall of Communism, the door was opened for Christian literature to be distributed in Russian orphanages. George was working in Russia with the International Bible Society. What he saw floored him and broke his heart. The kids were living in deplorable conditions. It was so cold inside the orphanage you could see your breath. Many kids were sick because of malnutrition, and they were starved for even a little love and affection. His burden was to help these children experience hope.

George learned some staggering facts about these kids after they no longer live at the orphanages. Sixty percent of the girls leaving the orphanages would end up as prostitutes, 70 percent of the boys would end up on the streets or in jail, and 15 percent of the children would commit suicide within the first two years out on their own.[5]

After returning to the United States, George knew he had to do something, anything, to help these kids. Because of the stage of life he and his wife were in, they couldn't adopt. But he asked God how he could be used to make a difference across the world in the lives of those who need so much.

George believed his greatest blessing from God was a strong, loving family. As he thought about that, he realized that what he could give—the seed he could plant—was a portion of the love he himself had received. Certainly he could help provide for the orphans' basic needs—physical, emotional, and spiritual—in the same way he provided for his two daughters.

So that's what he began to do. He invested his time, his talent, and his treasure in helping orphans. He told many of his friends about his vision, and together they started an organization called Children's HopeChest. Today, Children's HopeChest helps thousands of orphans across Russia and Romania every day, all because one man cared enough to take the little he had and give it to the fatherless.

Seeds for Today

Romans 12:1 encourages us to live transformed lives because of our commitment to God:

> *I beseech you therefore, brethren, by the mercies of God, that you present*

Being a living sacrifice starts with being sensitive to those people God brings to your attention.

your bodies a living sacrifice, holy, acceptable to God,
which is your reasonable service.

Being a living sacrifice starts with being sensitive to those people
God brings to your attention: single moms, widows, foster kids, the
homeless, and anyone you see hurting.

Here are just a few ways you can positively impact the lives of the
fatherless:

- Call an organization dedicated to helping orphans
  and become a personal sponsor. You can pick the
  age and gender of the person you sponsor, and you
  will receive a short history on your child. Children's
  HopeChest is one such organization: 1-800-648-
  9575 or visit www.hopechest.org.

- Befriend a child who is the member of a single-
  parent home. Take this child out for a soda or to
  an amusement park or concert. Be a mom or dad,
  brother or sister, to him or her for just a day at a
  time.

- Help a single mother. You probably know many of
  them already. Be a friend and help wherever you
  can. Watch her little ones once a week, help with
  groceries—be creative.

- Gather a group of friends and commit to place a
  small amount of your income, maybe 1 or 2 percent, into a fund that helps the fatherless. Choose
  trustworthy organizations that are helping the
  poor, and begin giving to a cause of your choice on

a regular basis. You may decide to support a good friend on the mission field or give to specific projects overseas, but whatever you do, begin giving.

- Write letters to an orphan overseas. (Children's HopeChest can help with this.)

- Find a widow in your community and offer to help in practical ways: Mow her lawn, run errands, or just invite her over for tea and visit with her. Be consistent in developing a relationship.

- When you hear of someone who is sick and who doesn't have any family close by, be his or her family—if only for a day. Take him or her some balloons, a get-well card, and a meal.

- Find out about foreign students who attend a local university. A great organization to help you connect with foreign students is International Students Inc. Contact them by calling 1-800-ISI-TEAM or by going to their Web site: www.isionline.org. Have students over for dinner. Maintain contact with them throughout the school year, and consider inviting them to share the holidays with your family.

- Become a foster parent. Look in the community pages in your phone book for the programs in your area. Most hold periodic informational meetings to help you find out what it means to be a foster parent.

- During the holidays, adopt a needy family in your community. But don't stop communicating when the holidays are over; make it a point to continue the relationship with the family year-round.

- Trade your usual family vacation for a mission trip. As a family unit, engage the fatherless and see not only what a change you can make in the lives of orphans, but also watch for the amazing transformations that can take place in your own family!

- Befriend someone who lives in the inner city or "on the other side of the tracks." Expand your peer group beyond those of your economic status.

- Volunteer at a local soup kitchen or homeless shelter. Do more than serve food; show you care by lending a listening ear.

- Next time you're in a long line at the grocery store, offer a genuine smile to the lonely-looking person standing near you.

- Organize a group to buy used cars, fix them up, and give them away to single moms and widows who need transportation.

> *Simple acts of kindness are all it takes to change a life, a community, even a nation.*

In the days ahead, the seeds you plant will sprout. They will grow tall and bear fruit for God's kingdom. Lush, rich life will return and replace the barrenness once found in hopeless hearts. You will be a hero because you took the time to be involved.

Simple acts of kindness are all it takes to change a life, a community, even a nation.

Want to start your own forest today?

NOTES FROM THE FIELD

Finances are usually a big issue with us single moms. We struggle to make ends meet, and I can't think of anyone who doesn't live payday to payday.

This summer was one of those times when I could actually breathe a sigh of relief about my money situation. I'd finally caught up, been able to pay all the minimum amounts due on my bills, and was just hoping nothing would derail me for at least a couple of months. Then, poof! Within two days I did get derailed.

My son had an asthma attack and the copays on the appointment and medication totaled $80. Then the next morning I got a phone call from a bed-and-breakfast I'd booked months previous as a surprise birthday present. I had totally forgotten I'd made the reservation, and they informed me that because I didn't show up, they had to charge my debit card. An unexpected, wasted, $120! I was mad at myself, down, and discouraged. Sunday came and went and then on Monday morning I went in to work and found a card on my chair.

I opened it and in it was $200 cash.

The card was one of encouragement, but it wasn't signed.

I was sure it wasn't from someone from work; they reported a female had dropped it off—someone whom they didn't recognize.

What a blessing! And for exactly the same amount I'd "lost." The fact that God would give back even when I'd made the stupid mistake of forgetting the reservation meant so very much to me. I was so filled with joy at the thought of it. Rather than let me live in the consequences of my forgetfulness, He laid it on someone's heart to give that much at that exact time.

It was a miracle.

Thank you—whoever you are—for listening and being willing to be God's hands extended.

—FROM A WIDOW, MOM OF FOUR

CHAPTER SIX

The Old Enemy, Fear

Have you ever wondered about the things that drew Jesus' attention when He walked the earth? What was it, more than anything else, that stirred His heart and caused Him to stop what He was doing and act on the moment? The answer is simple: another human being in need.

> *And seeing the people, He felt compassion for them,*
> *because they were distressed and dispirited like sheep*
> *without a shepherd.*
>
> (MATT. 9:36 NASB)

God's love was most tangible when Jesus noticed the defenseless. Jesus identified with those who were forced to live in misery and then he did something to relieve their pain. In Matthew 8 and Luke 17, Jesus

> *God's love was most
> tangible when Jesus
> noticed the defenseless.*

touched lepers—people the rest of the society declared as "unclean," as "untouchables"—and healed them. In John 4, Jesus reached out to an adulterous woman in Samaria during a time when men weren't supposed to talk to women in public—especially women with questionable lifestyles. In Matthew 19, when the disciples were rebuking people for bringing their children to Jesus to bless, He stepped in to say, "Let the little children come to Me, and do not forbid them; for of such is the kingdom of heaven" (v. 14). The character of our Savior is compassion.

Compassion Equals Involvement

Let's talk about compassion for a moment. Most of us would probably consider ourselves compassionate people. *Compassion* is one of those words that is supposed to characterize most everyone—*especially* in America. But if we really are compassionate people, why is humanity so filled with hate, violence, war, and oppression? Why are so many suffering from hunger and poverty, and lacking the basic necessities of life? Why are millions of human beings trying to cope with feelings of isolation, alienation, and loneliness?[1]

We have to rethink our understanding of compassion. What does it really mean to be compassionate, and how can we do this the way Jesus did? Is compassion merely showing kindness to those who are less fortunate than we are? Is it occasionally sending money to a charitable organization or donating clothes to a homeless shelter? While small actions can and do produce results, I suspect compassion—the way Jesus practiced it—means more than that.

I can't find a better definition of *compassion* than one Henri Nouwen gives:

> The word *compassion* is derived from the Latin words *pati* and *cum*, which together mean "to suffer with." Compassion asks us to go where it hurts, to enter into places of pain, to share in brokenness, fear, confusion, and anguish. Compassion challenges us to cry out with those in misery, to mourn with those who are lonely, to weep with those in tears. Compassion requires us to be weak with the weak, vulnerable with the vulnerable, and powerless with the powerless. Compassion means full immersion in the condition of being human.[2]

There you have it. Compassion is about *involvement*. To be compassionate means to get out of the boat of our current circumstances and get into the boats of those who are suffering. We are called to bear the burdens of those who are in need of companionship—to "weep with those who weep" (Rom. 12:15).

Look at how Jesus responded to those in need. It's almost as if the grimmer and more hopeless the circumstance, the more attention He gave it.

In Luke 8, Jairus's only twelve-year-old daughter had died. But Jesus stepped into the pain of Jairus's family and brought about new life by raising her from the dead.

In Luke 9, a man begged Jesus to heal his son, telling Him, "A spirit seizes him, and he suddenly cries out; it convulses him so that he foams at the mouth; and it departs from him with great difficulty, bruising him" (v. 39). Most of us would run from that kind of scene, but not Jesus. He walked *into* the distress, healed the man's son, and gave him back to his father.

> *Compassion means full immersion in the condition of being human.*

Is this true for us? Are we drawn by the daily needs of those around us? Are our hearts moved by the emptiness we see in the eyes of a recent divorcée? Do we recognize the pain of the business executive who has just been downsized into unemployment? Are we compassionate people? And more important, does our compassion compel us to act?

It's not easy to be confronted with the face of a fellow human being in desperation. I think of the countless times I have driven by a beggar on the side of the road or walked by a homeless person in a dark, dreary alley, never intending to lend a helping hand. In our minds, we walk through all of the reasons why we shouldn't help: "They would probably just use any money I gave them for drugs" or "You know, there are plenty of places for that person to get help if he wants it." But where is the compassion in those attitudes?

What if we translated this to the needs we hear about in other places around the world? Do we cry for the child in Honduras whose only source of sustenance is the trash heap he lives on? Does our soul ache for the infant who is abandoned on the side of a dirt trail in India, screaming for a meal from her mother, until she screams her last scream? Why doesn't our heart hurt more for those who are starving to death by the thousands, for children living in the slums because they have no parents, for young girls in Thailand sold into prostitution by their fathers for only a month's wage?

Perhaps sometimes these needs seem too remote, too removed from our lives. Most of us in the West can't personally identify with such suffering, much less think of ways to help. But so often we don't even help the woman across the street. We do nothing. Why?

The Padlock on Our Compassion: Fear

We don't help the beggar on the road or the single mother we know who is working herself to death for the same reason we won't help the orphan dying on the other side of the world. We flee from the need in front of us because of our ancient, ruthless foe: *fear*.

The fear of our lives being rudely interrupted enters into the equation of our desire to help. We think, *What if I become too involved?*

We are afraid of changing what we've always done. Our lives have become comfortable and manageable. If loving the stranger, the widow, and the poor have never been a part of our lives in the past—even if we

> *Fear is what prevents us from growing and changing.*

know it should be—it's always easier to keep things as they always have been. We don't like to rock the boat when the sailing is relatively smooth.

I've known so many people who feel they are called to give up their present lifestyle and follow Christ in missions or youth ministry or other service. But they're just too afraid. Others are intimidated by little things God asks them to do like becoming a volunteer helper at a weeklong summer day-camp for kids.

The idea may cross our minds to sign up to take a meal to the elderly widow who broke her hip last week. But then maybe we rationalize our lack of follow-through by telling ourselves someone else will do it.

What if these impulses are from God? What kind of joy might we be cheating ourselves out of?

Ironically, it turns out that fear is what prevents us from growing and changing. Fear wants nothing to change; fear demands the status quo. And the status quo leads to death.[3]

Who wants the status quo? It is stagnant and stymied living. Compassionate involvement is vibrant and fulfilled living.

But we have to muster up quite a bit of courage in order to overcome our fears. For me, this takes work! Reaching out to perfect strangers is frightening. I have to try hard to place myself among people who do this much more naturally. One such person who has helped me to overcome my fears is a fellow pastor named Keith Marvel.

Keith is one of those natural-born evangelists. Nothing scares this guy! One summer Keith had a great idea about reaching out to an entire apartment complex in a low-income neighborhood. He wanted me, as the youth pastor, to help lead it and involve the youth group. I agreed, but I was shaking in my shorts. When he decided we would go door-to-door to invite people, I told Keith I would do it, but only if he came along. (There's a good reason why Jesus sent out his disciples in twos. A lot of them were probably afraid like me!)

As Keith and I began to go around the complex and tell people about the BBQ and outreach we were having, doors of ministry opened up right in front of us. People asked us to pray for them about their drug

> *Most of His opportunities to care and heal occurred because He was out walking among them.*

addictions, and for their children who were sick. Single moms wept as we prayed because Jesus was making Himself real to them through our prayers. They begged us to come back. All we did was make the effort to go out and be open to the needs of those we met.

I'm reminded of a parable where Jesus asks us to "go out into the highways and hedges, and compel them to come in, that my house may be filled" (Luke 14:23). So many times we sit on our hands and wait for someone who needs help to come knocking on our door. That's the opposite of what we should be doing. Think of how many encounters Jesus had with the sick and with people who were possessed by evil. Most of His opportunities to care and heal occurred because He was out walking among them.

The results of that outreach weekend are still vivid in my mind. As the youth band played in the middle of the complex, dozens of people sat at tables and enjoyed food with the people of our church. The lives of those strangers were affected by love because we took the time to walk with them in their world. We gained a new perspective on giving of ourselves as we took the friendship of Christ out of the four walls of our church and brought it to those who were hungry for it.

When we left that day, those people knew what God's love felt like. And we knew reaching out was worth it because of the smiles on our new friends' faces.

Jesus: Compassion in Action

What is fear robbing from you? What kind of adventures in the kingdom of God could you be experiencing right now?

Perhaps you think you don't have the money—or maybe it's time you don't have to spare? The excuse doesn't matter; if fear keeps you from being who God wants you to be, the most important question you have to ask yourself is this: *Am I fulfilling the life I know I am called to live? Am I living my destiny?*

> *Am I fulfilling the life I know I am called to live? Am I living my destiny?*

The only person who keeps you from finding that kind of life is you. But you can change. We stop being dormant by taking the first step—by coming out of our safe place.

Fear didn't get in the way of Jesus living the kind of life He came to live. He made a life out of helping those who were most needy.

He still responds with love to the ones society has turned their backs on. Jesus knows that people—even the dirtiest and most unattractive people—are *the* most important things in life.

A story from Luke 7 offers a great picture of how Jesus treated people others typically looked down on. Jesus had been invited to have dinner at the house of a Pharisee named Simon. Remember, a Pharisee was a religious leader of that culture. They were the people who knew the Law and fulfilled it. At least, that's what they claimed.

As Jesus was dining with the "religious elite," a woman whom the Bible says was a sinner suddenly crashed the party and did something that was very socially unacceptable.

This woman approached Jesus and was unexpectedly overcome with emotion. She wept over His feet. When she realized Jesus' feet were covered with tears and those tears were mingled with the dust from the roads, she immediately began to dry them with her own hair! As if that wasn't enough, she began to kiss His feet. To top it all off, she broke open a very expensive jar of perfume she had been saving for her marriage day (probably worth a year's wages) and poured it all over His feet. We can understand a little about where this woman came from because it seems everyone in town knew she was a "sinner." At best, that meant she had loose morals. At worst, she was the town prostitute.

Somewhere in the recent past she must have had an encounter with Jesus. Perhaps it was on the side of the road as He as walked through town, or maybe it was a more private encounter when He took time to speak with her about the pain of personal issues. Whenever it was, she

> *She experienced love and forgiveness that healed her.*

experienced love and forgiveness that healed her. Her grateful response manifested itself during this Pharisee's dinner.

I imagine that she just wanted to thank Jesus for what He had done. Then the gravity of it must have hit her—being overcome by the fact that Jesus knew her sinful past and wicked way of life, and forgave her anyway. She wasn't "that sinner woman" anymore. She was forgiven and beloved of God. As she stood before Him, she lost control of herself, and the tears fell.

But when Simon the Pharisee—the one whose very religious vocation it was to be kind and compassionate—saw what she was doing, he made a statement that exposed his own sinfulness: "If this man were a prophet He would know who and what sort of person this woman is who is touching Him, that she is a sinner" (v. 39 NASB). In other words, if Jesus were the real deal, He would see through this woman, know she lived a sinful life, and send her away like the dog she was! Because of Simon's zeal to live a perfectly religious life, letting nothing unclean touch him, he missed out on so much. The sad part is that often you and I play the role of Simon. We hide behind our supposed goodness, when we're really afraid. Simon was scared to enter that woman's world. He feared their differences and what everyone might think. He did what too many of us do in the face of another's deep emotional response: Judge. Run. Ignore the problem. Pretend it isn't there.

Jesus could have been concerned about what everyone might say about this woman crying on His

> *Do something daring to experience the joy and blessing of loving the poor.*

feet. He could have worried about the rumors that surely would follow. He could have sent her away because her actions embarrassed Him. But instead He embraced her and valued her as much as anyone else at the gathering.

Today He uses us to show this same love to others—an unconditional love. This is the kind of love that doesn't fear what others think, doesn't fear a person's nationality, the kind of clothes he or she wears, car or house, but sees only the heart of a brother or sister and accepts that person right where he or she is.

How do we overcome fear? We start by making others' pain a priority in our lives. People are eternal; fear is not. We change our lifestyles and start to give sacrificially of our time, energy, and resources to the fatherless. And then we do something daring to experience the joy and blessing of loving the poor.

NOTES FROM THE FIELD

I'm forty years old. I never knew my real father. Can you believe at my age, I'm still suffering the pain of that loss? I wonder how many men there are out there like me?

Allow me to say a word of thanks. Your acts of kindness have helped me to see what a true godly man looks like. Being my friend, inviting me to dinner, asking me to go fishing: These simple acts have helped heal my broken heart. Now I have the courage to follow your example to my own children.

Your friend,

Steve

CHAPTER SEVEN

We Are All Cosmic Orphans

Perhaps as we've talked about the fatherless, you've seen an echo of your own life in these pages. Sometimes, in the stories of the hurting, we discover our own hurts. Their struggles are our struggles.

Whether or not we've truly been orphans, most all of us have felt at one time or another the way the fatherless feel. Certainly we've all experienced what it feels like to be a stranger. And during times of tragedy or loss, do you remember the pain and sense of hopelessness?

That's why our hearts naturally go out to the fatherless every time we hear about the pain they endure. It's our pain too.

The world we live in is full of questions. We all try to make some sense of them in order to understand the meaning of our existence. We struggle with existential issues such as, Who am I? Why am I so lonely?

Why am I having such a difficult time relating to others? Why do I feel hurt and abandoned by those who used to be my friends?[1]

Though the exact issues may be different for each of us, the root of the struggle is not.

Why Reach Out?

It's obvious that one of the reasons God calls His people to reach out to the defenseless is because they are the most needy. Without our help, they will die early deaths, they will be swept into lives of poverty, they will make bad decisions and end up in jail. The love of God's people can help them not end up as statistics. We can show them they have a chance to make it in life. We can be a turning point for them by making an effort to express the Father's love in simple ways that make eternal differences.

> *We're looking for what makes us whole.*

But another reason for reaching out to the needy may not be as obvious. Inside each of us, we're searching. We're looking for something that's missing. We're looking for what makes us whole.

Do you notice that we're never satisfied when we accomplish the next goal? The one thing we think will bring contentment or happiness fails to really fulfill once it's attained. Maybe it's only the *idea* of achieving something that makes it so attractive.

This truth should speak to you and me (and this is what it might say): Possessing things of this earth is merely an empty attempt to satisfy surface needs. In reality we have needs that run much deeper.

Cosmic Orphans

No matter what we have in this life, this fact remains: We are all cosmic orphans. We are looking for reasons to explain who we are and where we come from.

Have you known someone who was adopted? No matter how loving his or her adopted parents have been, deep questions about love and the very meaning of life persist in the minds of those who have been adopted. The past is a mystery longing for answers. An adopted person doesn't feel complete because a major piece of life is missing that might help explain his or her future.

I know what this feels like because I was adopted. I didn't know my real father for the first sixteen years of my life. I used to wonder, *Who is he? Am I anything like him? Does he feel the same things I do? Do I have habits that are like his? Would understanding more about him help to explain any of the problems I have in my life? Where can I find answers that will help me?*

We all want to have these

> We are all asking the same question: Who is my true Father?

questions answered, but the real need is to have them answered in the spiritual sense. The orphan, widow, stranger, and you and I are all asking the same question: *Who is my true Father?*

This same question must have been at the center of the disciples' panic when Jesus was about to be taken away to be crucified. This group of rough-and-tough, full-grown men were frightened because Jesus was talking about leaving them.

Why were they afraid? Because they had built a relationship with this astonishing person—this person who had revealed to them the loving heart of God. Jesus had given them a new perspective on life and answered many of their deepest questions about who they were, where they came from, and where they were going. Like adopted children who have searched for a parent, they had found their true Father through Jesus.

But He said he was leaving. How could this be? What would they do? Who would be the brother, teacher, and friend they'd come to depend on? Who would be there to show them the Father's heart?

When the disciple Simon Peter asked Jesus where He was going, Jesus answered, "Where I go, you cannot follow Me now; but you will follow later." Peter probably spoke for the whole group when he cried out in desperation, "Lord, why can I not follow You right now?" (John 13:36–37 NASB).

Take a look at how Jesus responded:

> *Let not your heart be troubled; believe in God, believe also in Me. In My Father's house are many dwelling places; if it were not so, I would have told you; for I go to prepare a place for you. And if I go and prepare a place*

for you, I will come again, and receive you to Myself, that
where I am, there you may be also.

(JOHN 14:1–3 NASB)

Jesus encouraged and comforted them, letting them know He was not abandoning them. He was going to take care of things for their future, and He was coming back. And then Jesus spoke right to the very heart of the matter:

I will not leave you as orphans; I will come to you.

(JOHN 14:18 NASB)

Why did He use the word *orphan*? Because that's exactly how they felt—and that was exactly what they were until Jesus came on the scene and revealed God's love.

Through Jesus' love for them, the disciples had begun to understand and know their true Father. He showed them what life was about and how to live it. They were no longer orphans. They were the children of God!

This is the greatest need each of us has—to know our true Father. Knowing Him brings definition, fulfillment, and completion to our lives. It truly answers the questions of our existence, yesterday, today, and tomorrow.

God is our Father. Paul assures us of this same truth in the book of Romans:

You have received a spirit of adoption as sons by which
we cry out, "Abba! Father!"

(8:15 NASB)

That word *Abba* literally means "Daddy." I used to wonder why we use that term to refer to God.

Now I understand. It's because the greatest cry of my heart is to know my true "Daddy." When I know I belong to Him, my feelings of abandonment fade away. I know I am loved unconditionally. I have a purpose for living, and the One who desires to be with me more than any other will parent me as a perfect Father should.

> *When I know I belong to Him, my feelings of abandonment fade away.*

The Spirit Himself testifies with our spirit that we are children of God, and if children, heirs also, heirs of God and fellow heirs with Christ. (ROM. 8:16–17 NASB)

We inherit what Christ inherits. We are full-fledged, card-carrying children of the Father!

We are all created in the image of God. Our greatest desire is to be singled-out, cherished, and loved in a way that makes us feel like we are significant. Nothing could give us more confidence in this truth than hearing the voice of God saying to us,

> I have called you by name, from the very beginning you are mine and I am yours. You are my beloved. On you my favor rests. I have molded you in the depths of the earth and knitted you together in your mother's

womb. I have carved you in the palm of my hand and hidden you in the shadow of my embrace. I look at you with infinite tenderness and care for you with a care more intimate than that of a mother for her child. I have counted every hair on your head and guided you at every step. Wherever you go I go with you, and wherever you rest I keep watch. I will give you food that will satisfy all your hunger and drink that will quench all your thirst. I will not hide my face from you. You know me as your own as I know you as my own. You belong to me.[2]

Where has this journey led us? To a treasure chest filled with countless gifts. Remember the places you have traveled and people you have met in these pages. And as you continue down this road of ministering to the fatherless, realize there is still a wealth of treasure to be discovered. This is just a beginning. The more we become the hands, the feet, and the love of Jesus, the more joy we will find. When we give, we end up receiving much more than we could ever imagine.

After all is said and done, when we sincerely ask God the question "If I could live my life doing only one thing, what would You want me to do?" I believe the message of Isaiah 58:7–9 (NIV) would be His answer.

Is it not to share your food with the hungry,
And to provide the poor wanderer with shelter—
when you see the naked, to clothe him,
and not to turn away from your own flesh and blood?

Then your light shall break forth like the dawn,
and your healing will quickly appear;
then your righteousness will go before you;
and the glory of the LORD will be your rear guard.
Then you will call, and the LORD will answer;
you will cry for help, and he will say: "Here am I."

He *is* here … with you.

As you walk through the fields of the fatherless, your light will break forth like the morning, and the life you live will no longer seem mundane and meaningless. Instead, every minute will be filled with joy, purpose, and significance.

When this life is over and you stand face-to-face with the Father, what a reward will be in store for you!

Because you saw the face of Jesus in the face of the lost and lonely, God will see His Son in your eyes.

Because you cared most about what He cares most about—God will recognize you as His faithful partner.

And because you made every effort to express the Father's love, even the smallest deeds you did for the least of these will count greatly for all eternity.

CHAPTER EIGHT

Working the Fields

And so we come to the end of the book, but it isn't the end of the story. For many of you, it will be the beginning of a grand, exciting story—one filled with joy and blessing.

I want to leave you with just a few stories from the field. May their stories inspire you to walk boldly into the fields of the fatherless, offering God's love to those who long to be loved!

They Cry for a Father

Bill and Elaine Jones's Story

Elaine: Orphanages don't usually let foreigners see their soon-to-be-adopted children unless the family is far along in the process.

Well, when we were in Ryazan, Russia, we asked anyway if we could see (Kelsey) Valeria interact with her peers, and they said yes. I peeked in at a room of twenty toddlers all sitting in groups of four at tiny tables as they sat to wait for their meal. The children saw me, took a little interest, and then went back to talking amongst themselves.

Then it was my husband's turn to peek in. As I sat in the outer room, I could hear the children's voices. They were repeating the same word over and over again and kept getting louder and louder. I soon realized that the word that they were saying was "Papa." I had to see who they were talking about. As I looked in, my husband passed by me, walking out the door with tears in his eyes. The children were calling to my husband with arms outstretched.

"Papa!"

They see women everyday, so when I peeked into the room, they took little notice. But when my husband appeared, they were suddenly reminded of the person they longed for in their lives.

They longed for a father. A daddy.

A Change of Heart

Ray Johnson: I met a Russian Orthodox priest in the small town where our orphanage is located and decided to develop a relationship with him. It didn't take long to discover he didn't have a very good opinion of the children in the orphanage. His only previous exposure to them was at the police station.

It soon became my goal to help him see that these children had worth. During one of my visits, he mentioned some work that needed to be done around the church. I recommended a couple of the more reliable boys from the orphanage. He dismissed the offer because "it would take more people to supervise them then the work they would do."

I did not give up. Instead, I encouraged the orphanage director and the shop teacher to intercede with the priest as a means of giving the boys a chance. But it was the Holy Spirit who really did the interceding!

A year later while I was visiting, the priest told me what a help the boys were and that he was mentoring one of the boys about important life decisions. I also learned that two girls from the orphanage were helping his wife plant flowers around the church.

Today his children play with like-aged children from the orphanage. Some share meals with his family. Now that the priest has become a champion of the children, I can only hope and pray that the townspeople will also come to accept them as the worthy people they truly are.

Luda's Journey

Jerrilyn Billings: When I made a commitment to go to a Russian orphanage called Holuy, I didn't know how much this experience would change my life. During my stay, I met the most incredible children and staff, along with the beautiful people of Russia. Even though their situation was dour, their smiles and spirit showed me that God was already at work. I was so lucky to have met the boy I'd begun to sponsor and the other children. But one little girl, Luda, stood out to me. She clung to me like Velcro and we spent all six days totally attached to each other. Her smile, her beautiful eyes, and her incredible hugs would bring me such great joy each day. When it was time to finally pack up and leave, I was heartbroken that I would have to leave her.

After returning home, my heart was heavy, and each passing day grew more difficult because I could not hold Luda. Day after day I prayed and asked God how I could possibly bring her home, knowing that it would be so difficult for me with my own situations in life.

Almost a year later when all seemed lost, I was at work walking by the front counter. Benji, a contractor I have worked with, asked me, "Hey, Jerri. Didn't you go to Russia last year?"

"Yes, I did, and it was the most amazing experience ever," I replied.

"My wife and I are adopting a little girl from Russia. Would you believe that I saw your picture in a little photo album while we were there?"

My heart stopped and so did everyone else who was witnessing this. The only way he could have seen my picture was if he had visited the same orphanage where I was almost a year before. In my excitement I started asking who they were adopting. At first he couldn't remember her name but the moment he mentioned her eyes I knew. It was my Luda. My dear, sweet Luda, whom I had been praying for all this time. My knees about buckled and everyone around me was celebrating. Neither Benji nor I had any idea the other had been to Russia until that moment.

Within four months of our conversation, Benji and his wife, Tiffany, brought Luda home. They decided to change Luda's name to JourNee to remind them of their incredible experience. She was no longer halfway around the world—she was just minutes away from where I lived!

Within a few weeks of their return, Benji brought JourNee to visit me at work. What a reunion it was. There wasn't a dry eye in the house. We were witnessing and embracing a true miracle.

More Than Just a Bigger Family

Aimee Davis: In 2001 our family was the image of the traditional American family: father, mother, son, and daughter. We had no idea of the plans God had for us.

In response to the desire to grow our family, I began learning all I could about international adoption. In the fall of 2001 we moved forward with the adoption of a baby boy born in Guatemala.

As the airplane lifted from the runway in Guatemala City, I held our baby boy tightly and cried tears of intense joy and sadness. My joy was a celebration of the beginning of Marco's new life with us. But there was also sadness in my heart for the circumstances that caused Marco to begin his life as an orphan.

Since bringing Marco home, we have welcomed another brother, Gustavo, and a sister, Ana Lucia, to our family. The traditional American family with one son and one daughter has now grown into an American-Guatemalan family of five children!

Loving our three Guatemalan-born children is easy. Addressing the circumstances that placed them in our family is the challenge. In our children's birth country 75 percent of the population lives below the poverty line. Chronic malnutrition remains a grave problem for 50 percent of Guatemalans. Out of 100 Guatemalan children, 5 will not live to see their 5th birthday, 28 will never learn to read or write, and 95 will never enter high school. Our family has chosen to respond.

I have visited Guatemala 11 times in the last 5 years. We have identified organizations in Guatemala that are making a difference and support them financially and, more importantly, by working alongside them. I have traveled to Guatemala alone, with friends, and even with our teenage children to serve those in need. My teenagers and I have volunteered in orphanages, libraries, and feeding centers in rural villages. It has been an amazing privilege to watch my kids minister selflessly to those in need.

When our family began the adoption journey, we had no idea that our oldest would jump on a trampoline at an orphanage with children hungry for love and attention. We never envisioned our daughter cuddling babies who did not have the loving touch of a mother. I doubt we would have believed our older children would one day play soccer with a group of boys at an orphanage.

We believed we were simply growing our family. God had so much more in store for us. He was creating a heart for serving those in need. He was creating a compassion for orphans. He was creating a new ministry for our family. Our goal is to mirror the example of Christ. Life has taken on new meaning in serving the needs of the people of Guatemala.

Lord, Please Give Me Strength

Dustin Froelich: My heart was racing as I stepped off the bus and gazed through the rusty gates of the orphanage in Pokrov, Russia, that would become my home for the next two weeks.

I had heard for two years about how our church in Colorado was helping this orphanage. Thanks to our donations they had working bathrooms, clean water, better food, a computer lab, musical instruments, and an overflow of loving letters from sponsors. After learning so much about them and seeing their pictures in church, I wanted to meet these kids.

But as I walked through the intimidating gate, my excitement turned into fear. What did I get myself into? How will I get around the language barrier? What if they don't like me? My self-defeating thoughts were interrupted as someone grabbed my hand and urged me to pick up the pace. I looked down to see a young boy, maybe eleven or twelve, looking as excited as can be, speaking to me in Russian as though we'd been best friends our whole lives. I tried to explain to him that I couldn't speak Russian, but the boy I came to know as Sasha did not seem to mind. After a first-class tour, I promptly met all his friends and found that they were very interested in play-fighting, break-dancing, and soccer. I was in for the workout of a lifetime. Words were quickly replaced by sound effects as we reenacted scenes from movies and video games.

My apprehension left as quickly as it came, and I found myself acting like a child without a care in the world. Until this point in my life, I never thought much about my height. Apparently sitting on the shoulders of a 6'1" guy is the place to be. Besides, with one kid on my shoulders, the others had the rare opportunity to play-fight a two-headed monster and be the hero of the hour. The first day flew by, and as I lay in bed that night to gather my thoughts, exhaustion took over, and the only prayer I could muster was "Lord, please give me the strength to do this again tomorrow."

After breakfast on day two, I thought of a game to teach the kids to get them to trust me. I had one of my American friends demonstrate as he closed his eyes, held out his arms like airplane wings, and fell backward. Standing a few feet behind him, I caught him just before he hit the ground. The kids were impressed and quickly formed a line eager to try. It was around lunchtime that I learned this game is easy to do a few times but very difficult to do hundreds of times in a row. Shortly thereafter, I had one kid on my shoulders, one hero on my back pretend-slaying the two-headed monster, and one kid falling in front of me, much to my surprise, with his arms wide out expecting to be caught. My prayer for that day? "Lord, I'm not sure if it is okay to pray for superhuman strength, but if it is, I could really use some now." I caught the kid; God is good. Oh, here comes the next one! And another! That night, climbing into bed was difficult—my legs wanted to give out. Again, the only prayer I could manage before falling asleep was "Lord, please give me the strength to do this again tomorrow."

I was the best human jungle gym I could be for the next two weeks. My arms became monkey bars, my legs became a slide, my shoulders became a lookout … I even think I was a pirate ship at one point! As I played with the kids, I had one goal in mind: Never tell them "Not right now, I'm too tired." I knew I had two weeks with these kids, and I was determined to spend every second of every day loving them, teaching them, laughing with them, and connecting with them.

My time in Pokrov was a glorious blur. Time stopped at the orphanage. Nothing in this world mattered beyond the walls and trees sheltering us from the outside. I forgot that I lived on the other side of the world. I forgot about my car, I forgot about my clothes and my home. I forgot about eating out at restaurants and talking on my cell phone. I forgot about bills and global warming and politics. I think I even forgot that I didn't speak Russian. For two weeks I had one task to accomplish: Love these kids. That was it. Life simplified.

An Extraordinary Story

Janie Van Dyke: Daniel Perez Pineda was born in Colombia on December 11, 2004, and weighed only 3.5 lbs. He immediately became available for adoption as a child with extraordinary special-placement needs. Why? Daniel was missing all of his limbs. In April 2005, I received an e-mail from Isabel, Bethany Christian Services' facilitator in Colombia asking if I could find this baby a family. If so, she would send me his photo. I hesitated, wondering if I could really find a family who would accept a child with such significant needs. Reluctantly, I asked Isabel to send the picture. But once I saw Daniel's face, I knew I could find him a home. My job is to find families for children with special-placement needs.

I immediately sent out an e-mail with Daniel's photo and information to Bethany's branch offices and to my list of prayer warriors. I then sent information to Brittany's Hope Foundation, a nonprofit foundation dedicated to aiding and facilitating adoptions of special children from around the world.

On the same day I sent Daniel's information to Brittany's Hope, a woman named Charlotte Holmes called me. Charlotte told me about her family and their desire to hear more about Daniel. Charlotte and Greg Holmes had already adopted internationally: Their daughter Anna was from Guatemala, and Jasmine, born with spina bifida, was from China.

After much talk and prayer, Greg and Charlotte submitted an application. With Bethany's approval, the couple sent an acceptance letter to Colombia. Colombian adoption officials approved the Holmes family for Daniel's adoption. Thanks to Bethany's office in Madison Heights, Michigan, the home study and paperwork were finished in record time! The family left for Colombia on August 29, 2005.

With help from Brittany's Hope Foundation, Bethany's Caring Connection Fund, a reduction of Colombia's adoption fees, a reduction of Bethany's fees, and the gracious donation of our Colombia staff of their time and efforts, Daniel's adoption was fully funded!

A team of medical experts in East Lansing, Michigan, recently met with and evaluated Daniel (renamed Zeke). They will decide what prosthetics, if any, will be appropriate for him. The team doctor anticipates that Zeke will eventually require help only with special tasks, such as dressing himself. She envisions a time when Zeke will become nearly self-sufficient.

Charlotte sent me this update recently that captures the blessings of the Holmes family:

"Zeke is thriving in our family and amazes us daily by finding new ways to do things that people with arms and legs take for granted. He is truly a blessing, and we ask ourselves daily what we did to deserve such a blessing. He adjusted so well that it feels like he has always been with us. He is very happy and delights us with smiles and giggles on a daily basis. He says 'Dada,' which melts his father's heart every time he hears it. His sisters adore him and love playing with him and making him laugh. We are so in love with him that our hearts have swelled with joy, gratitude, and thanks to Bethany Christian Services and Brittany's Hope Foundation who made it possible for our little bundle of joy to come home."

The Price of Obedience

Paula Pittman: In June 2006, I obeyed God's call to go to a small village in Russia and bring God's love to a group of orphans. I have had the privilege of serving in other missions in the United States and around the world, but until 2006, I had never spent a week totally dedicated to investing in the lives of orphans, sharing God's love with them.

After twenty-four hours of travel and one short night of sleep, we rolled into the orphanage. We were ushered into a room and given a warm welcome by the orphanage director and the psychologist, who works there and is the heart of the orphanage. A few minutes later, we heard the footsteps of children walking down the hall, coming to meet their new American friends. As I heard those footsteps, tears began rolling down my face. I hadn't even seen the sweet faces of these children, but God put a love in my heart for them I knew He wanted me to share with them for the next seven days. That is exactly what I did. Never before in my life as a believer have I felt as if I was simply a vessel for God's love to pour through. The trip was not about me in any way. It was only about these fifty-six precious children.

I have made three trips to Russia to minister to these children. My days and nights are filled with the thoughts of the orphans we now call our own, the caregivers and teachers who love these children and dedicate their lives to them, the discipler who goes to visit them regularly and teach them of God's love for them, and the wonderful translators who have also become like family.

There is a price to pay for being obedient to God's call to care for the fatherless. The price is your heart. The heart that was once mine no longer belongs to me. It belongs to the children in Holuy whom God has graciously shared with me, and to every orphan in the world. What an honor to be able to be used by God to let these children know that they no longer need to fear because their heavenly Father has them in the palm of His hand.

A Softened Heart

Wendi Shelton: About two years ago, I was sitting at my church listening to Tom Davis speak on the plight of the Russian orphans. I was on the edge of my seat. The video that followed his message moved me to tears. One of the girls in the video reminded me so much of my daughter, except that instead of planning for homecoming and learning how to drive, this girl was telling us what "hell" was like—because she was living it as a Russian teen orphan recently turned out on to the streets. As I sat watching, I knew I had to go. I had to do something. Go where and do what? I wasn't certain—but I felt a deep stirring in my heart like I had never felt before. After church that day, I decided to sponsor a Russian orphan and also signed up to go on my first short-term missions trip—to Russia. I had no idea what I was getting into, but I never once doubted the decision.

When I told my friends and family, no one was surprised that I was going on a short-term mission trip. They were, however, surprised I was going all the way to Russia—and even more surprised that I would be serving in an orphanage with young children. I was not naturally a "kid" person. But God had a different plan for me.

The girl I was sponsoring at the time of my first trip to Russia (who has since been adopted) was in preschool. So God in all His wisdom (and perhaps because of His sense of humor) sent me across the world to work with preschool children. To stretch me even more outside my comfort zone, He had me doing crafts with special-needs preschoolers. God used me in a way I could never have imagined and would never have chosen on my own. My heart was softened as I reached out to these kids every day.

I learned about selflessness. Tenderness and mercy became a part of my being as I held hands, hugged, patted, kissed cheeks, and stared lovingly into lonely, cold, haunting eyes. I learned patience for children who don't speak our language, who have disabilities, who cling to you, who can't express their feelings or frustrations, who find it a challenge to tell us their "favorite things." And I learned the true meaning of friendship when my sponsored girl—Anya—hugged me on our last day with tears streaming down her face and saying, "I was looking for a friend, and I found one in you. I will be drowning in drips tonight."

On the last day of my most recent trip (I have been there three times, now), I wandered onto the playground and found a boy all alone on a swing in the far corner of the yard. I motioned for him to come and join our group for a game of catch. A few of the kids in the circle shook their heads, and he shook his head. Something moved me to go to this boy and start pushing him on the swing. He smiled, so I kept pushing. As I continued pushing him on the swing, I told him my name. I told him he's my friend, and he nodded. After a couple minutes he got up from the swing and started to walk away. He looked back at me with a smile on his face. Then he came back and touched my arm, and I realize he was "tagging" me. He wanted me to chase him—it's the kids' favorite game. I chased him around the playground a few times, and then he found a Frisbee and threw it to me.

As he walked away, I realized that I didn't know his name. How long had he been playing by himself? I felt shame for not knowing his name. But, you see, this was my God moment. Because as of that day, he is no longer a face in the crowd or a boy without a name. Sasha has a name, and now he has a voice. God loves Sasha and all the children of Holuy more than any of us can.

As we boarded the bus our last day, I looked for Anya's face in the group. I wanted to see her face one more time, but I was also afraid I would have to turn away. I found her at the end of the line—the kids had lined up against the fence to wave good-bye. As I saw her tears and felt mine, I realized that only God could form a bond like this. Only

God could create so strong a relationship between an adult and a child who were complete strangers less than a week ago. I love her in a way I could never have imagined.

God softened my heart; I listened and obeyed. And now, everyone who knows me knows who Anya is.

A GUIDE TO WALKING IN THE FIELDS OF THE FATHERLESS

Want to go deeper into the fields of the fatherless? This guide will help. Use it as a personal study or invite members of a small group to join you as you explore the ideas and questions below.

Chapter One: The Fields

Guiding Question: How can you incorporate the Fields of the Fatherless principle into everyday life?

1. As a family or group of friends, make a decision to be the church in action. Here are a few simple suggestions to assist you:

- Celebrate a birthday party as a party in honor of orphans. When my son, Hayden, turned seven, all of his friends brought presents for a group of orphans. We notified the parents we were doing this and explained why and provided clear instructions. The presents were sent to a needy child overseas, and we received pictures of them being delivered. It was a tangible expression of how to love the fatherless.

- Take a mission trip together. Sign up to feed the homeless on a weekend or holiday. Or, instead of Disneyland this year, find a great mission organization and take your whole group on a trip to serve widows, orphans, and the poor.

- On a night you would normally go out to dinner, do something different. Send the money you would have spent at a nice restaurant to a worthy cause along with a note explaining why you are doing this. Exercise the spiritual discipline of fasting on this night if that's appropriate for your family. Here's a fact to help you as you consider this idea: We think little of spending $5 on a fancy coffee: a hazelnut latte, cappuccino, or something similar. In many African countries $5 will pay for 100 meals. A little sacrifice on our part can go a long way.

- Connect with a local organization that works with
  the fatherless domestically or internationally. Ask
  them for a project you could take on that will
  make a significant difference in the lives of people
  in need.

2. Edwin Burke, the British philosopher and statesman, once said, "The definition of evil in the world is when good men and women see injustice and do nothing." Good and loving people hear about the cry of the orphan, the plight of the widow, the hunger of the poor, and they shut their hearts. They pretend it isn't happening and it doesn't affect them.

  a. Where have you heard of evil winning the battle
     and done nothing? Examine your heart and ask
     for forgiveness. Now make a commitment to
     never let it happen again. The strategy to win
     over inaction is action!

  b. What needs do you know of that you could
     meet? Think of someone in your community
     who's in need, then reach out and be a catalyst of
     change.

3. God loves and cares for those who are suffering. Rent or purchase one of the following movies to align your heart with the people who are on God's heart. Watch it, then spend time thinking about what it meant

to you. Many of these are available at your local video store. (This activity is perfect for small groups. Watch one or more of the videos together, then spend time discussing them. Use this as a springboard to action!)

- *Emmanuel's Gift*—www.emmanuelsgift.com

- *Dear Francis*—
  www.chronicleproject.org/dearfrancis/film.html

- *The Invisible Children* (not appropriate for young children)—www.invisiblechildren.com/themovie

- *Children of Leningradsky*—
  www.childrenofleningradsky.com

- *God Grew Tired of Us*—
  www.godgrewtiredofus.com

- *The Orphans of Nkandla*—(You can purchase this video and other documentaries at www.truevisiontv.com.)

4. Use these questions for personal reflection or small-group discussion:

Why do you think God is so concerned about what happens to the stranger, the widow, and the orphan?

Who are these people today?

How can you apply the Fields of the Fatherless principle to other aspects of your life?

What specific things can you do to bless the fatherless?

Is it easier to minister to those who are like us or to those who are different from us? Why do you think this is true?

In what ways may God bring blessing to your life because you help those in need?

Chapter Two: The Fatherless

Guiding Question: How can you be more present in the lives of the fatherless in your community and around the world?

1. Justice is an issue God raises over and over in the Bible. Martin Luther King Jr. understood the absolute necessity that God's people fight for justice. In fact, he gave his life for it. From a jail cell in Birmingham,

Alabama, in 1963, he wrote, "Injustice anywhere is a threat to justice everywhere. We are caught in an inescapable network of mutuality, tied in a single garment of destiny. Whatever affects one directly, affects all indirectly." None of us can afford to let injustice slide by and hope it goes away. We are all in this together.

Do a biblical word study or topical search on justice and injustice. A great place to start is www.biblegateway.com. Using the concordance in your Bible works too. Then think about what you discover, and spend time in prayer asking God to help you know how you can be a champion of justice.

2. Pastor Rick Warren of SaddleBack Church in California believes that the whole business of Christianity is going into "the sores of life," helping those who are helpless, hopeless, and hurting. "If we don't do that," he says, "I doubt our Christianity." Watch the one-and-a-half-minute clip called "Why the Church Must Care" at http://www.saddlebackfamily.com/peace/hiv_aids_initiative. Make a list right now of what the "sores of life" are in your hometown or state. Then write down what you're going to do about it. Design a plan and execute it.

3. If you have a story of fatherlessness in your own life, write it down. Perhaps you're a single parent. Maybe one or both of your parents was emotionally absent from your life. Telling and then seeking understanding of your story is the best road to healing.

4. Spend time with someone you know who has been affected by father-lessness or tragedy. Have them share their story. Ask them questions about how they would have liked someone to reach out to them. Then pray a prayer of blessing over their lives.

According to Scripture, gratitude is the key to having a compassionate heart. Our hearts get dry and callused when we are unthankful, and that spills over into other areas of our life. Take a few minutes and tell God what exactly you are thankful for.

5. Use these questions for personal reflection or small-group discussion:

Who are some of the fatherless you know today?

What are some ways you've reached out to the fatherless? Have you felt God's blessing for doing that? What was that like?

In what ways can you help bring justice to the fatherless?

What are some of the ways you can offer one of your "two tunics" (see Luke 3:11) to help those in need?

Chapter Three: What Does God Look Like?

Guiding Question: If Jesus identifies Himself as actually being "the poor," how can you find Him?

1. Mother Teresa once said, "The dying, the crippled, the mentally ill, the unwanted, the unloved—they are Jesus in disguise…. [Through the] poor people I have an opportunity to be 24 hours a day with Jesus…. Every AIDS victim is Jesus in a pitiful disguise; Jesus is in everyone…. [AIDS sufferers are] children of God [who] have been created for greater things."[1]

What is your immediate reaction to this quote? How does it impact the way you see those who are suffering? What does it do to your heart?

2. Write about an event in your life where you saw God. Maybe it was like the one I had when I helped the woman who had fallen out of her wheelchair. Did you sacrifice financially to help someone else? Did you go on a mission trip that changed your life? Describe in detail what happened.

3. After you've finished describing your "God encounter," write down exactly how you felt while it happened and after it happened. Get in touch with how powerfully this event changed your life.

4. Think of specific ways you can minister to "the least of these" (Matt. 25:40, 45). Don't just think of giving money to a beggar or helping at the local homeless shelter. These are good things to do; just don't stop there. What about starting a ministry to single parents at your church? What if you helped mobilize families in your church to partner with the local Human Services agencies that place foster-care children in foster families? Consider recruiting a team from your church to minister to orphans in Russia or China. Or lead a team to Africa to help AIDS orphans. Anything is possible with God! Once you have a vision for making a difference, write it down. Make it as clear and concise as possible. Now create a strategy to make this vision a reality. How will you do it? What pastor would you recruit to help? What families need to be on this team? How will you print a brochure? Who will you recruit? Don't worry if you don't have all the answers. Take a leap of faith, and God will meet you to make up the difference!

Chapter Four: The Blessing of Adoption

Guiding Question: How does God's adoption of us as recorded in Scripture impact your personal understanding of adoption?

1. Interview someone who has adopted a child. Seek to learn as much as you can about the adoption process and the realities of raising an adopted child. Then spend lots of time in prayer with that person (or

entire family) thanking God for all He has done and asking for blessing and wisdom in the years to come.

2. Use these questions for personal reflection or small-group discussion:

Why do you think God chose the path of adoption to welcome us into His kingdom?

What does it feel like to know you've been adopted by God? Is it something that you resonate with, or is it a foreign concept to you? Explain.

What does it mean that adoption is "the visible gospel"? Describe your answer in detail.

If you're not called to adopt a child, what are other ways you can be involved in the adoption process or to help others in their pursuit of a son or daughter?

Chapter Five: Seeds of Hope

Guiding Question: We've all been impacted by the "seeds" others have planted in our lives. After reflecting on those seeds, how can we continue to be seed planters in the lives of others, particularly the fatherless?

1. Planting a seed, even a small one, is a powerful way to change the world. Jean Giono changed the world. If you watched the movie *Emmanuel's Gift* suggested in the study questions for chapter 1, you realize how *any* person, can change the world. What story or stories can you think of about people who have made a huge impact on society? List these people and briefly describe their stories. Consider doing research to find out more about the seeds they planted and how those seeds made a difference in the world.

2. One of the best ways we can positively impact the fields of the fatherless is by using our influence. Make a list of all of the people you know you can recruit to join you in this fight for the fatherless. I know widows in their seventies who have recruited their entire churches to sponsor an orphanage; teenagers who have recruited and led thirty people to conduct an inner-city children's camp for three days; and children who have rallied entire Sunday school classes to supply a retirement center with flowers and the *Jesus* film! Use your influence to make a difference. What can you do?

3. What other ideas do you have? Perhaps you or someone you know has done something we haven't yet thought of to try. Please log on to www.fieldsofthefatherless.com, and tell us your story about what seeds you have planted and how they have grown into greater things!

4. Use these questions for personal reflection or small-group discussion:

Who, in your life, has sown seeds that have made a tremendous impact on you? What did they say or do? What gifts did they bring? How did they treat you?

What are the seeds that have been planted in your life and how are they bearing fruit?

What are some seeds you've planted in others' lives?

How can you go about planting seeds in the lives of the fatherless?

Chapter Six: The Old Enemy, Fear

Guiding Question: How can you overcome the barriers of fear in your life and act on what God is calling you to do?

1. The key to defeating fear is action and involvement. Keep in mind that even Jesus didn't minister to every single need that crossed His path. He listened to the voice of His Father, and He acted on what He heard. Ask the Father what He's calling you to do in this area of ministry. Take a moment and unlock your heart. What's that inner voice saying your responsibility is in these fields. Is it to write a book? To go back to school and get a degree in cross-cultural missions? Adopt a child in need? The question isn't if we should be involved in the fields of the fatherless, it's how.

2. Make a list of people who will support you in your new endeavor. Who comes to your mind? Who will be supportive? Who will love you through the difficult times and the great times?

3. Invite these people to your home or meet them at a coffee shop to share your vision. Let them see your heart and passion. Then ask them if they will join you and support you with their influence, their prayers, their time, or whatever it takes to launch what God is asking of you.

4. Be honest about the areas in your life that could prevent you from accomplishing your goals. What fears and apprehensions do you have?

What obstacles tend to stand in your way? What character traits do you need to exhibit in order for this to succeed? Now take some time to go over each of these areas in prayer and turn them over to God. Ask Him to help you defeat these fears. Break their power in the name and authority of Jesus! Once you expose them, you have power over them. Fears love to hide in darkness; they can't stand the light!

5. What can you sacrifice right now as a tool to defeat fear, as an offering to God as it says in Romans 12? Read that chapter, specifically verses 1 and 2. Should you sacrifice food for a period of time and fast? Should you make a financial sacrifice (perhaps a gift to a ministry that helps the poor)? Should you approach your pastor about starting a ministry even if you're feeling inadequate? Make a sacrifice to the Lord and make it now!

Chapter Seven: We Are All Cosmic Orphans

Guiding Question: What practical difference does it make in your approach to ministry when you think about the fact that we're all "cosmic orphans"?

1. Henri Nouwen wrote a book called *The Wounded Healer*. In it, he discusses how we've all been wounded by people and circumstances.

The key to healing is to turn our wounds into agents of healing in the lives of others. Take a close look at your past wounds by writing them down or discussing them in a loving community. Then be proactive by creating a plan of how you can share your wounds with others in order to bring healing to their lives and to yours.

2. Many of us spend the majority of our time living for earthly things. Some of these things are necessary, and others are simply distractions. Make a list of things that are time wasters in your life. How many hours a week do you spend on those activities? Now make a plan to turn those hours into hours that count for eternity. How can you reapportion those hours for the kingdom?

3. One of our primary struggles as Christians is sorting through the worldly voices that whisper in our ears. These voices try to tell us who we are, what we're supposed to do, and what to fear. Expose these lying voices by verbalizing what they're saying and praying against the authority you've given them over your life. What does the voice of your true Father say about you? Listen to that voice and write down what you hear Him saying about your future, your gifts, and your calling. Set aside a time of meditative reflection to listen to God's voice through Scripture. You will discover emerging patterns in these two experiences. Make this a part of your normal prayer time.

4. Take time to think about what your inheritance in the kingdom of God will be. Matthew 25 reveals that all of us will be standing in heaven

receiving that reward. "I was hungry, and you gave me something to eat; thirsty, and you gave me something to drink ..." Who will be there to say thank you to you for feeding them, clothing them, and giving them something to drink? Process the gravity of this truth and discuss how to keep ministry to the poor at the forefront of everything you say and do.

NOTES

Chapter One

1. UNICEF.com, "Who are the Invisible?"
www.www.unicef.org/sowc06/press/who.php (accessed January 31, 2008).
2. Sheryl Henderson Blunt, "Bono Tells Christians, Don't Neglect Africa," *Christianity Today*, April 22, 2002, 18.
3. F. W. Boeham, *The Heavenly Octave* (Grand Rapids, MI: Baker Book House, 1936), 18.

Chapter Three

1. Malcolm Muggeridge, *Something Beautiful for God* (New York: Harper & Row Publishers, 1971), 22.

Chapter Five

1. Ken Gire, *The Weathering Grace of God* (Ann Arbor, MI: Servant Publications, 2001).

2. Press Release cb98-228.html, U.S. Census Bureau, www.census.gov, 29 April 1999.

3. "American Agenda," World News Tonight with Peter Jennings, 12 January 1995.

4. Open Doors Statistical Survey, 13 November 2001, www.opendoorsweb.org/Press/International_Students_in_the_US.htm.

5. The National Summit, Atlanta, Georgia, November 2000—The CoMission for Children at Risk.

Chapter Six

1. Henri Nouwen, *Compassion: A Reflection on the Christian Life* (New York: Image Books, 1983), 4.

2. Ibid.

3. Jean Vanier, *Becoming Human* (Mahwah, NJ: Paulist Press, 1998), 73.

Chapter Seven

1. I am infinitely grateful to Ravi Zacharias for these ideas. For further study on the struggle to finding meaning and understanding these existential issues, please consult Ravi's book, *Can Man Live Without God* (Dallas: Word Publishing, 1994).

2. Henri Nouwen, *Life of the Beloved* (New York: Crossroads Publishing, 1992), 30–31.

A Guide to Walking in the Fields of the Fatherless

1. Edward W. Desmond, "A Pencil in the Hand of God," Time.com www.time.com/time/reports/motherteresa/t891204.html (accessed February 4, 2008).

Also available from Tom Davis and David C. Cook:

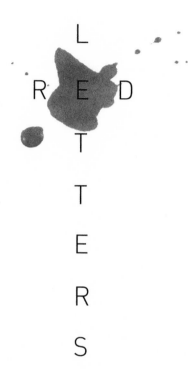

L
E
R   D
E
T

T

E

R

S

LIVING A FAITH THAT BLEEDS

Chapter 1 excerpt

Go and do the same.

—Luke 10:37

A LIVING GOSPEL

RUSSIANS CELEBRATE THE arrival of spring in March. During a Russian spring, temperatures hover just above freezing during the day, which melts the graying snow—only so it can freeze again into a world-covering sheet of ice at night. There are no tiny blooms reaching up through the earth to try to touch the sun. No patches of green to add color to the bleak landscape.

It was one of these spring nights when ten of us were walking down a dark, icy sidewalk in Vladimir. A young boy darted across the street, heading straight toward us. He was twelve, maybe thirteen, dirty and wearing tattered rags. He was speaking Russian. Asking for something. Pleading, perhaps.

"Sorry, we don't understand," we said. It was no lie.

But we did understand the voices inside our heads that spoke with equal measures of cynicism and sad resignation. Just another worthless beggar. If we gave him money, he'd probably spend it on drugs or cigarettes. If the kid really wanted help, there are plenty of shelters that could feed him and offer a place to sleep.

We kept walking. But something inside fought to quiet the voices. Something inside challenged me to act in a way consistent with the Savior I follow.

I turned, grabbed the translator by the arm, and went back after the boy. "Hey! Come back." *What do I say?* I thought. *Where do you begin to reach out to someone in need?* "What's your name?" I asked. "Kak tibya zavoot?" Dema, my translator, repeated in Russian. I got down on one knee so we were eye to eye.

"Kirill."

He was no longer just a beggar on the street. He was a little boy with a name—a name shared by a Russian Orthodox saint. I looked into his eyes. He had a story to tell. A story filled with pain and heartache. A story marked by hunger and homelessness. He was shivering. Somehow he'd survived the cold Russian nights.

Just a little boy.

"Hi, Kirill. My name is Tom. How can I help you?" Dema translated for me with a rapid-fire smorgasbord of Russian words.

Kirill had run away from a dangerous situation. He hadn't

eaten in three days. He looked so frail standing there. All he wanted was a place to stay and some food.

"Would you help me?" he asked.

That stupid voice went off in my head again. The same voice that speaks to me when I happen upon a panhandler back home in the States. *He'll probably just buy vodka if we give him money.* That inner voice—it's mine. And it very well could be speaking the truth. But it's not the voice I want to hear. I want to hear Jesus. Did he put conditions on the help he offered? A familiar story elbowed its way past my hesitancy. A story of Jesus helping a woman caught in adultery. Jesus didn't refuse to help the woman because she might sin again. He forgave her and told her to sin no more. She was worth the risk. She was worth helping.

"Kirill, here's money for food and a bus ride." We gave him the address to the ministry center for Children's HopeChest. There he would find help. We made arrangements for him and told the staff we would pay for whatever he needed.

Kirill took the money and walked off into the black night, fading into the distance like a ship on an uncertain journey.

I wondered what Jesus felt as he watched those he helped walk into the night. Did all of them live changed lives? Did they all stop sinning? Did they all hang on to the hope they had been missing?

About an hour later we received a phone call from the ministry center. Kirill had arrived and was receiving the care he needed. They would find him a place to live. Somewhere safe.

My cynical inner voice was silenced. I had only offered money for food and bus fare, but it was Jesus who had spoken to Kirill.

He didn't need a translator to hear Jesus' words now. Kirill was tasting them in a meal. Feeling their touch in the comfort of a warm blanket. And resting on them in the hope and promise of a good tomorrow.

He was just a little boy.

And on that cold spring night in Vladimir, Russia, he was Jesus.

You may be wondering, *Was that a typo? Didn't Tom mean that he, Tom, was Jesus to Kirill?* Of course we're called to be like Jesus. Colossians 3:10 (NIV) tells us to put on the new self, which is being renewed "in the image of its Creator." This is the basis of our spiritual formation, something Paul taught about with great passion and wisdom. And, yes, reaching out a helping hand to someone in need is one way we live out that Christlikeness.

But there is something else going on when we reach out to help the helpless—something unexpected. Something we often miss. Something that speaks not only to the process of becoming Christlike—to our spiritual formation—but also to the very truth of where we find Jesus.

LOOKING FOR JESUS

I've discovered a new way to live. Every morning when I get out of bed, I look for Jesus. No, not because I've misplaced him. And I'm not talking about a feeling I get during prayer, or revelation that comes to me while reading Scripture. I'm talking about finding Jesus in the eyes of real people. In the eyes of the poor, the handicapped, the oppressed, the orphan, the homeless, the AIDS victim—the abandoned and the forgotten.

Throughout Scripture, Jesus identified with the poor in amazing ways. He was their champion, their advocate. He gave them purpose and meaning and hope. He held them in high esteem and blessed them. There is something deep and meaningful about this. In Matthew 25:40, Jesus said, "Whenever you did one of these things to someone overlooked or ignored, that was me—you did it to me." Was he truly saying that we will find him in the lives of the poor? This is a rich mystery.

We shouldn't be surprised. Our God is indeed a God of mystery. Isaiah 55:8–9 says,

> "I don't think the way you think.
>> The way you work isn't the way I work."
>> God's Decree.
> "For as the sky soars high above earth,
>> so the way I work surpasses the way you work,
>> and the way I think is beyond the way you think."

You don't have to read very far into the New Testament before running head-on into one of the greatest of these mysteries. I don't know about you, but I (and more than a few Jews in Jesus' time) would have expected the King of the universe to be born in a palace—someplace worthy of his status. He would have slept on no less than four-hundred-thread-count Egyptian cotton crib sheets and rested his head on a down-filled, silk-wrapped pillow. The mobile above his crib would surely have been crafted of sparkling gems—white diamonds, red rubies, blue sapphires, and green emeralds. And all of the most respected people in society would visit this beautifully decorated nursery to worship him.

But that's not how God did things. Jesus was born in a dirty, smelly, disgusting barn. He was laid not on a clean sheet but in a manger—a feeding trough filled with animal snot and drool and their leftover half-eaten food. He wasn't welcomed to the world by great leaders, by rulers and officials and other members of the Lexus-drivers club. He was met by a bunch of lowly shepherds. Yes, three kings or wise men arrived from the east months later. But nobody even knew who they were.

Are you getting the picture? Jesus didn't come to earth and identify with the rich, the successful, and the most influential. He entered the world as a pauper. He entered the world not in the comfort of his parents' home, nor in the company of smiling relatives or even the safety of a hospital. He arrived in the humblest of places, in the lowliest of circumstances. God hid the mystery of the kingdom in the lives of the most needy.

Is it any wonder, then, that Jesus associated himself with the "least of these"? That when we help them, we're helping Jesus? God has tremendous love for those who are rejected, abandoned, and laughed at. This truth came clear to me when I started reading about the life of Mother Teresa. Read what she said:

> The dying, the crippled, the mentally ill, the unwanted, the unloved—they *are Jesus in disguise*.... [Through the]

poor people I have an opportunity to be 24 hours a day
with Jesus. Every AIDS victim is Jesus in a pitiful disguise;
Jesus is in everyone.... [AIDS sufferers are] children of God
[who] have been created for greater things.[1]

In some crazy way, Jesus *is* the poor. When we find the "least of
these," we find him. If this doesn't turn your theology upside down,
I don't know what will.

There's a story told about an incredible transformation in an
old monastery because people lived out these truths. M. Scott Peck
recounted the story in his book *The Different Drum.*

The story takes place in an orthodox monastery in eastern
Europe, sometime in the early twentieth century. The monastery
was in danger of being shut down. For centuries it had been the
house of a great monastic order, but after hundreds of years of
persecution, and in an age when many people believed orthodoxy
was no longer relevant, the abbot and four monks found themselves to be the last members of the order. The branch houses
were long gone, and even in this one remaining location, the five
monks hadn't been successful in attracting new members. Each of
these monks was over the age of seventy. It didn't take a mathe-
matical genius to see that the order was doomed. This caused the
monks a great deal of worry and anguish, but they remained
faithful: Every day they diligently, if sullenly, carried on their
work.

In the deep woods surrounding the monastery there was a little hut that a local rabbi occasionally used for retreat and

contemplation. One day it occurred to the abbot to ask the rabbi if he had any advice on how to save the monastery.

When the rabbi saw the abbot coming up the path, he went out to greet him. But when the abbot asked his question, the rabbi could only grieve with him. "I know how it is," he said. "The spirit has gone out of the people. It is the same in my town. Almost no one comes to the synagogue anymore." The old abbot and the old rabbi wept together. When the time came for the abbot to leave, they embraced each other.

"It has been a wonderful thing that we should meet after all these years," the abbot said, "but I have still failed in my purpose for coming here. Is there nothing you can tell me, no piece of advice that you can give me, that would help save my dying order?"

"No, I'm sorry," the rabbi responded. "I have no advice to give. The only thing I can tell you is that one of you is the Messiah."

When the abbot returned to the monastery, his fellow monks gathered around him to ask, "What did the rabbi say?"

"He couldn't help," the abbot answered. "We just wept and read the Torah together. He did say something as I was leaving— something cryptic: 'The Messiah is one of you.'"

In the days and weeks and months that followed, the monks pondered this and wondered whether there was any significance to the rabbi's words.

The Messiah is one of us? Could he possibly have meant one of us here at the monastery? Which one? Do you suppose he meant the abbot? Yes, if he meant anyone, he probably meant Father Abbot.

After all, he's been our leader for over twenty years. But if he meant Father Abbot, why didn't he say so? He might have meant Brother Thomas. Thomas is so gentle and kind; we all know that he's truly a holy man.

Certainly he didn't mean Brother David! David gets so crotchety. Then again, even though Brother David is a thorn in our flesh, he's nearly always right. Exceedingly right.

Well, the rabbi couldn't possibly have meant Aloysius. Aloysius is so passive, a real nobody. But he does have a gift for always being here when you need him. He just magically appears by your side. Maybe Aloysius is the Messiah.

Well, I know one thing for sure. The rabbi certainly didn't mean me. He couldn't possibly have meant me. I'm just an ordinary person. But what if he did? Suppose I am the Messiah? Oh God, I pray that it's not me. I wouldn't know how to be the Messiah.

As they contemplated in this manner, the monks began to treat each other with extraordinary respect on the off chance that one among them might be the Messiah. And on the off, off chance that each monk himself might be the Messiah, they began to treat themselves with extraordinary respect.

Because the forest in which it was situated was beautiful, people occasionally visited the monastery to picnic on its tiny lawn or to wander along some of its paths. As they did, without even being conscious of it, they sensed an aura of extraordinary respect that radiated from the monks and permeated the atmosphere surrounding the monastery. There was something strangely attractive, even compelling, about it. Hardly knowing why, people began to come back more frequently to picnic, to play, to pray. They brought friends to show them this special place. And their friends brought their friends.

Some of the younger folks who came to visit the monastery started talking with the monks. After a while, one asked if he could join them. Then another. And another. Within just a few years the monastery had become a thriving order and, thanks to the rabbi's cryptic gift, a vibrant center of light.

Does this story sound familiar? It should. Both the Old and the New Testaments tell similar stories—taking care of strangers, caring for those in need, and treating others like they could be angels in disguise.

LITTLE CHRISTS

You may be asking, "Well, what other way is there?" There have always been *two* ways. C. S. Lewis wrote, "The Church just exists to help people be little Christs." I certainly have met individuals and church families who live this out. But all too often, those of us who call ourselves Christians live in direct opposition to what Christ said we should do.

Living out the gospel is hard work. It's easy to talk about it. Any of us can sit in church and sing warm, happy worship songs that make us feel good. We can nod agreeably with the pastor's wisdom. And sometimes we can even drop a few extra dollars into the offering basket. But it's not so easy to actually go and *do* what Jesus said to do.

Jesus calls us to live in ways that go against our natural inclinations. For example, I don't have the easiest time living out this verse: "I'm telling you to love your enemies. Let them bring out the best in you, not the worst. When someone gives you a hard time, respond with the energies of prayer, for then you are working out of your true selves, your God-created selves" (Matt. 5:44–45).

Frankly, I want my enemies to burn. I want them to suffer for the wrong they did to me. I want revenge. That's my initial response. My human response. But because I have been redeemed by Jesus' sacrifice, the truth of the living Christ who is ordering my life challenges that response. I (sometimes slowly, often painfully) embrace that truth and learn to say no to my human response and yes to what Christ wants me to do.

Most of my life I have prayed that these sorts of transformations would occur almost magically. That I would wake up one day and be a totally different person. That all of my desires would be godly. That I would have a natural inclination to deny myself, pick up my cross, and follow Jesus. That I would suddenly just love my enemy. But it didn't happen like that.

Transformation *did* occur when I would hear the words of Jesus and obey them, no matter how I felt. The more I obeyed, the more I was transformed. I was becoming a different person because I was *living* myself into it. I was becoming the words I saw on the page. The words Jesus himself spoke.

What if all Christ-followers lived the Red Letter words in the Bible—Jesus' words? What if we offered the hungry something to eat, gave one of our many coats to someone who was cold, and truly loved *all* our neighbors as ourselves? How radically different would our lives be? How different would our *world* be if Christians were really living as little Christs?

That's what this book is about. Learning to live a faith that is so real, you bleed Jesus. Here's how to start: Look for Jesus every morning in the eyes of the people you meet. And then look for him in the mirror.

Thanks for joining me on this journey through the fields of the fatherless. If you have any thoughts or words you would like to share, or if you would like me to speak at your church, group, or organization, please contact me at tom@fieldsofthefatherless.com or 719-487-7800.

I'll look for you in the fields of the fatherless!

Join Tom in the fields of the fatherless. Turn what you've read into action by being Christ's hands and feet through many opportunities with Children's HopeChest, a leader in international orphan care.

GET CONNECTED

ENCOUNTER the living Christ in the fields of the fatherless. Join us on a vision trip. Call us for more information about our next vision trip to Africa or Eastern Europe.

JOIN the 5 for 50 Campaign. Children's HopeChest is proud to participate in the 5 for 50 campaign—5 practical ways to make a positive impact in the lives of nearly 50 million people suffering from AIDS worldwide. Go to **www.5for50.com** and make your pledge to help orphans in Africa. You can make a difference for as little as $5/month.

VISIT www.hopechest.org to find out more about how you can care for orphans through the programs of Children's HopeChest.

CONNECT OTHERS

INVITE your pastor. We believe in this so much that we offer pastoral scholarships as an investment in your church's ministry to orphans. Call the outreach team at Children's HopeChest.

STAY CONNECTED

READ Tom Davis' Blog. Tom regularly visits Russia, Africa, and other places around the globe. He updates his blog regularly with videos and reflections on his experiences, and shares current information on orphan care. **www.cthomasdavis.com**

DRINK Saint's Coffee. With every pound of this fair trade and organic coffee purchased, you will feed an orphan for a month. **www.saintscoffee.com**

800.648.9575 • www.hopechest.org

CHILDREN'S HOPECHEST
Confidence to fly and a safe place to land

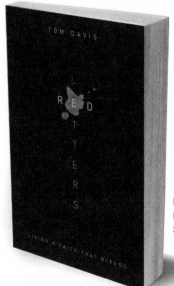